Climbing is this yin and yar  ¹ when
to back off can be the diffe   ]
failure. And, never forget ¹   1
like floating anyways, a prc
doing. Like love. Becoming one with som...

Travis,

Thanks for all the

years of real friendship.

Its not everyday you

meet a kindred, true friend

& from early on I knew

we had that. Peace & love

brother. Enjoy the stories,

Wu-tang forever

peace,

Luke

"Luke Mehall's writing explores the unglorified realities of the American dirtbag climber. Never sugar-coated, his is a raw and at times painfully honest questioning of and reflection on climbing, life and loneliness; a soulful voice that somehow brutally and with an undeniable authenticity gets to the nub of things.

Reading American Climber reawaked my love of climbing literature. Mehall's books are modern classics, I believe his writing heads a new and exciting wave of climbing literature."

Tom Randall, of the Wide Boyz

"Luke Mehall emerged as a writer just in time to chronicle the dwindling light of the soul-climber: one who climbs for the aesthetics, who adventures for the freedom not the recognition, who's hi-tech gear is merely a tool rather than a totem. Luke and his cohorts embody the dream of the American West with all its promise of freedom and risk and reward. To dive into a Mehall book is to be brought along on a ride that we all wish we had the courage to board, but most of us trade that courage for comfort."

Chris Kalous, host of the Enormocast podcast

"Luke Mehall is one of the few adventure writers out who handle the tricky first person voice as if it were made for him."

John Long, climbing legend and Senior Contributing Editor, *Rock and Ice*

"Who's more in tune with the ethos of the dirtbag—and more able to write passionately and honestly about it—than Luke Mehall? I think no one."

Brendan Leonard of Semi-rad.com, and author of 60 Meters to Nowhere and New American Road Trip Mixtape

"Luke Mehall brings the abstract realm of personal transformation back down to earth."

Georgie Abel, climber/writer/poet

Graduating from College Me

A Dirtbag Climber Grows Up

by Luke Mehall

Cover design by Mallory Logan (www.go-roshambo.com)

Cover photo: self portrait of the author (left) and Dave Ahrens on the Moonlight Buttress, Zion National Park, Utah, circa 2005.

Chief editor: Lindsey Nelson (www.exactedits.com)

This book is dedicated to Shelley Read, a college professor of mine, who showed the same passion and interest in my life and writing when I was "college me" as she does today.

Yeah, the ones that you're calling wild

Are going to be the leaders in a little while

This old world's wakin' to a new born day

And I solemnly swear that it'll be their way

You better help the voice of youth find

"What is truth?"

—Johnny Cash, "What Is Truth?"

Author's note:

"Do you ever just run out of words?" a person asked me during an interview recently.

The reporter was asking me questions about my third book, *American Climber*, a memoir I wrote about how climbing saved my life. The answer was a definitive absolutely not. Personally, I feel like I have more ideas of things to write about than I do time to write. The words and ideas are coming at an infinite rate.

It wasn't always this way, for the first ten years of my writing career, I didn't actually write all that much. For a lot of this time, I was on the road, climbing and, to be honest, kind of lost. Here's an excerpt from *American Climber* describing a time period in Joshua Tree, California, that perfectly describes that era of my life:

I knew I was blessed with the opportunity to live a good life in America. Perhaps I knew it too much, because I was willing to live with such little money it astounded everyone back home in Illinois. I figured money would always be there, and I could simply work and earn it if I really ever needed to, and that is a blessing, a confidence that the man who has never had money could never have.

The why I was there I could have never understood at the time. I wanted to climb would have been my answer. The weekend warriors who frequented J-Tree would always be jealous of me when I told them how long I was staying for. That would immediately make them think of work on Monday, and they would think of me climbing on Monday. I would carry that aura of living the dream in our conversation, but it was an illusion. There was just so much that was missing. If it really came down to it, I was as jealous of those people as they were of me. Jealous of their significant others, their stability, their jobs, well, maybe not their jobs, but I was jealous that they had a life plan set into action.

And therein lived my battle, my struggle. I was out in Joshua Tree because, after eighteen years of schooling, I still didn't know what to do for a career. I didn't want to fight, I didn't want to teach, I didn't want to research, and I didn't want to study in classrooms anymore. I felt like I was given a world of opportunity, and I still passed on every opportunity except that opportunity to climb rocks and live outside.

I'm grateful I stayed with the writing path, because I learned that just simply climbing rocks and working as little as possible in service-industry jobs would not make me happy. Eventually, I realized that if I simply continued to do that, I would become miserable and crusty.

So like many dirtbag climbers before me, I grew up. I became a legitimate writer and worked on the craft every day I wasn't climbing. I also sought out the security of a reliable vehicle, a roof over my head, and health insurance; in short, I was no longer a hardcore dirtbag living hand to mouth. If something went wrong climbing, as it often does, I would have a backup plan.

As I chose the fork in the road that involved some security, many of my friends went down the same road—they got married, became professionals in their fields, and had children. Life became richer, and more well rounded. And, most of us were still climbing a lot too; we didn't forget what made us who we are today.

As I grew up and became more responsible, I realized there were personal and spiritual sides of my life that I'd neglected for many years while just rambling or on the road. In short, I realized I needed to grow up and work on various aspects of my life that I'd ignored for many years. Here, in *Graduating from College Me*, I tried to write about those struggles and successes in an honest way.

This book was written in the same style as my first two books of short stories, *Climbing Out of Bed* and *The Great American Dirtbags*. There's a little more poetry in here than anything I've ever published—lately, I've been more inspired to write poetry than ever before; after all, it is the purest form of writing.

—

The last few years of balancing a career, relationships, and the never-ending drive to climb have been the richest of my life. I've also had several friends pass away during this time period, and their departures are a reminder of how precious life is and how quickly it can all pass by.

Thus, the answer remains to live in the moment, love with an open heart, and always stay committed to growing into the best person I can be. This book is a meditation on those thoughts, and stories that, I hope, show a commitment to growth. I also hope you'll appreciate the random, fun stories in this book as well.

Lastly, I must express that the journey beyond the simple dirtbag life is still full of setbacks and obstacles. Know that my existence is still defined by the beautiful struggle that is life, and I'm fighting for love, my self, the stories, and to not be overtaken by my demons.

I thank you for reading, and I hope you enjoy the book.

Word.

Luke Mehall
Durango, Colorado
Summer 2016

Twenty-Four Hours of Vegas

The best thing about America is that it gives you space. I like that. I like that you buy into the dream, it's a lie but you buy into it and that's all that matters.

—Chimamanda Ngozi Adichie, *Americanah*

As a traveling modern vagabond in my postcollegiate years, I would always end up in Las Vegas. I was lured there by the climbing in Red Rocks, and inevitably my comrades and I would end up partying in Sin City. Thus, "Twenty-Four Hours of Vegas" was born.

Inspired by a liberal arts education, coupled with the belief that I could live out of a tent and always be happy, I was a dreamer. I dreamed of the open road. I dreamed of climbing forever. I dreamed I'd find myself out there somewhere in America.

Sometimes, as a solo road dogg (that's right d-o-g-g), I would arrive in Las Vegas alone, and alone is the best word to describe that feeling. I had a penchant for gambling, and I would park my car and then walk to find the cheapest casino. I'd have a couple drinks, walk alone down the Vegas strip, and after miles of walking, find the cheap, sad casino at the end of the line, where dreams go to die. Now, why I never started right there at the sad, cheap end, I'm not quite sure. Las Vegas is full of illusions—maybe I thought I'd gamble a little where the people with money did and win big.

Of all the times in my five years wandering from climbing area to climbing area, with the hopes of finding myself, or simply finding something, these were the moments I felt the saddest and loneliest. I don't think I was necessarily sad about my own life but sad about the human condition there. Especially the old folks, those who smoked cigarettes and played slot machines. There were too many to count, and to peer into their empty souls, when I was in these days of hopefulness and openness that life could be beautiful, was simply too much to take.

But I looked—I looked at Vegas and took it all in, similarly to when I was out in nature, studying a climbing area, and drinking in the vastness of the wild. I studied Vegas too much, like looking into the sun too long. I'd been warned. I'd read Hunter S. Thompson's *Fear and Loathing in Las Vegas* and knew enough that Vegas was where the American Dream went to die. I knew the town was started by mobsters. I knew that, environmentally, this place was on borrowed time; a place that consumed so much water, energy, and resources was out of place in this desert. But, I was there, and I would drink it all in.

I was a college student in the George W. Bush 9/11 days, a fact that shaped me more than I probably realize, even nearly fifteen years after the event. In college, I was upset about the war, upset about the conditions of the environment, and upset that the world was an unjust place. Some people go to college and figure out what they want to do for a career. After graduating from a liberal arts college in the middle of the mountains in Colorado, I only knew what I didn't want to do, and that was to be a part of the sheepish American mainstream.

So, this was where I was. Of course, I was full of contradictions, and though I was a college graduate, I was a freshman in life. I made my living by washing dishes and living in my truck. When the work dried up in the seasonal mountain town, I drove said truck across the United States and Mexico and slept in the back. I was going to be a writer, but I'd yet to truly write much. I was searching.

Red Rocks was one of my favorite climbing areas. It was a featured, forgiving array of pink, red, and maroon sandstone, juxtaposed with the sprawling Vegas landscape. When you awoke just before the sun prior to a big multipitch climb, you won at life—you won because there were so many others losing, still awake from the night before, partying, searching to feel, perhaps sinning so much they would hardly ever recover from such transgressions. I didn't know much at this time, but I knew it felt good to do good. And, climbing all day, that was good.

Of course, I liked to party too. I was young. I'd ruined more than one climbing trip to Vegas by celebrating before I had anything to celebrate. A hangover leading up to its name—the partying hung over my head as I sweated in the hot desert sun, my simple sinning dripping over, spilling onto a cactus, and I stumbled through the desert, begging my climbing partner to retreat from our planned mission.

And, this was why we came up with Twenty-Four Hours of Vegas. We would climb a big two-thousand-foot route, Epinephrine, by getting up early, and then stay awake through the night until we'd been awake for twenty-four hours straight. Plenty of outdoor events were centered on the theme of exercising for twenty-four hours; we'd just throw in a little partying for good measure.

We awoke in the dark and quietly exited the industrial BLM campground, an ugly area set on the edge of this beautiful red rock world. Soon enough, the sky was pink, a sunrise that felt a little man made, the light pollution and smog mixing with the beauty of Mother Nature's sunrise. And, we headed into the canyon.

We are the climbers of a new age, the age when climbing exploded in popularity. My generation knows no difference; we don't know the era when climbing was an underground culture, before there were climbing gyms in every city and bolts on every crag. We do know a simple rule: you have to get up before they do. We needed to be the first people on the climb.

We were also a party of four. We needed the space and time to move fluidly together up the two thousand feet of stone. After thirty minutes of hiking up a drainage into Black Velvet Canyon, we arrived at the base of Epinephrine, relieved to be the first ones racking up for the climb.

Years ago, we'd been snaked by another party at the beginning of the climb; we were racking up at the base, and they scrambled up forty feet above us to the right and snuck up into the route, forcing us to wait until they got higher. They only got a hundred feet up and then decided to bail, to rappel. By the time all this ensued, we lost our interest in going up; they'd killed the vibe with their unsportsmanlike manners.

But, as the sun came up this day, creating a pink sky, we looked above to a massive chimney system and knew we had our chance. There was no one was above us, and we were the only ones at the base of the climb. It was ours for the moment.

We climbed in two parties of two—myself and Mark, and Tim and Tim. The nervousness of a rushed morning turned into solid, efficient movement up the chimney system. It was featured and forgiving, and we set a good pace to be successful on what would be one of the longest climbs I'd ever done.

I could bullshit and embellish, but I don't actually remember the vivid details of the climbing that day. My mind's eye can recall the chimney, and that once it was over, there was a nice ledge with maybe eight to nine hundred more feet of climbing, moderate featured climbing that seemed to go on forever.

His sister, Jane, searched for him for years; given that he was a professional gambler, many theories existed on his whereabouts. His sister was relieved when DNA tests revealed that the remains were his. I had the chance to speak to Jane a couple times on the phone, while we brainstormed ideas for a story that never took shape. She wasn't a climber at all, but she loved her brother, and she cherished the legendary stories about him and all his adventures and new routes. Even though the story never came to fruition, to listen to her talk about her brother put so many things into perspective. As climbers, danger and risk become routine; it's good to be reminded that our lives are on the line, and we risk it all for this thing we love.

Epinephrine gave me a dose of what I love the most about climbing, being way high off the deck with a thousand feet or more of air below your body. Such exposure puts you deeply into the moment. And those moments are gone once you reach the belay and stop. Gone forever. Sometimes makes you wish you didn't have to stop and belay. But on the end of the rope is your buddy, and it's nice to share those moments.

All four of us made it to the top just as the sun was going to bed. We didn't dream of rest and sleep at that point—we dreamed of more; Twenty-Four Hours of Vegas was happening! The hike down was a little complicated, a series of having to make the right decision about where to go. Fortunately, Tim and Tim had climbed Frogland, a route just adjacent to Epinephrine and had scoped out the descent. We stumbled for a while, maybe an hour and a half, until we were back in the canyon. The light of the Luxor blazed into the sky, seemingly showing us where the next step of the night was. We emerged out of the wash, back at the truck.

And then we drove into Vegas. We ate some fast food, just as the place was closing down for the night. We dreamed of partying, gambling, and karaoke. Tim was a karaoke king and could rock the house with some AC/DC or Vanilla Ice.

Somehow it didn't occur to us that it was Sunday, and by the time we got downtown, it was midnight. We wandered the strip and put money in slot machines and did the things people do in Vegas. We drank beer openly, as you can there, and made jokes and screamed, Twenty-Four hours of Vegas.

We kept wandering and wandering, and I found a karaoke place where I once performed the MC Hammer dance in front of a hundred people. I'd told Tim about this, and he was superpsyched to check the place out. But, once we found the joint, it was closing for the night. We looked in like we'd missed something. The time for fun on the weekend had passed. But we had to make our twenty-four-hour mark so we wandered some more. We got on a shuttle train and rode it back and forth several times, all of us falling asleep at one time or another. Finally, four in the morning rolled around, and we called it a day. The most sober of us drove back out to the Red Rocks campground.

It could have been just another Vegas trip, where people take their sinning to a certain level that they are comfortable with, or go beyond it and regret it. In those days, my heart was hungry, and my soul was yearning. I believed in doing good, and probably more importantly, doing what feels good and will still make you feel good the next day. Climbing was exactly that, and the part that made me feel the best in those twenty-four hours was the climbing. Sometimes, I try to imagine dealing with my hunger and my angst without climbing, and I simply can't do it. Places like Vegas would have swallowed me and spit out a weak man.

I haven't been to Vegas in some time now. Inevitably, it seems to be a central place in the West for a climber; it's easy to end up there. These days, with all the water issues, I often wonder if we'll see the demise of Sin City. I always did think Red Rocks would be much more appealing without Vegas right next to it. Who knows though, if the city did collapse, surely some seedy characters would still persist in the remains. We humans sure are resilient, for better or worse.

Like the famous statement by René Daumal in *Mount Analogue* about the climber always having to leave the summit, yet he still knows the glory about the heights above him because he has been there—the same applies for Vegas. Alone, I felt the sadness of this island of sinning. I still know that desperation, the sadness of someone nearing the end of their life, alone, looking into a slot machine for some sort of salvation, or maybe just looking into that, cigarette lit, because they gave up long ago. You can't dwell too long on the sadness of things you had nothing to do with creating though; this world's full of too much of it.

So, I cling to the joy, those moments with friends, like that day on Epinephrine, feeling like we won at life because we could experience such freedom in a free experience. Because in one twenty-fourhour time period, I stood thousands of feet above Vegas and realized that high up on a perch is the best place to be, where wonder and amazement dominate. And later in that day, I also experienced the doldrums of America, that one telling you all America's gimmickry will make you happy. Knowing too, the answer to happiness in America is not so simple, and it lies somewhere in between the ether, the mountains, and civilization.

An Indie Publisher's Poem

Love…
You're seeking it
And writing it
Searching for it

And you wrote this book
From your heart
And every nook and cranny
Labored it over years
Thought about it over beers

And then you set to pitch it
You thought it was the shit
Or at least fit to be published
But none of the publishers listened

One editor even said
It won't be read
You've got no narrative
It won't be well received
You know what you need to do
She said

Is chop it up
Sell excerpts to the magazines
And then, I started to bleed
She might have well said
To slit your wrists
To deconstruct my dreams
To sell it to magazines
People don't even read anymore
Like they used to

So in e-mail
I didn't cry
I simply replied

"fuck your couch"

In the nicest way possible

And decided to publish
The damn book
Independent style

(Those unaware of the phrase "fuck your couch", from Dave Chappelle, should head over to YouTube and search those words.)

A Confrontation with Racism

In my writing, I shy away from controversy and lean toward the warm fuzzies. I enjoy writing things that make people feel good about what they are reading, regardless of whether we share the same viewpoints on environmental, social, spiritual, or political issues.

Recently, something happened that I simply have to write about: a racist comment. It was late night, two in the morning, and I was at the home of some close friends. There were some people I didn't know as well, but as it goes it Durango, new faces often become new friends. Then the comment happened. It was about black people. I looked across the room to see if anyone was as offended as I was, and sure enough my buddy spoke up and said, "I have black people in my family."

The guy followed that up with another racist comment. My buzz was instantly killed, and my blood boiled. I was absolutely shocked to think that a person within my circle of friends could be so blatantly racist. I mean, after all, it is 2013, and we've had a black president for over four years.

Later, I talked about the event with my friend who spoke up. He offered, "Man, I'm from the South and used to racism, but to say something like that here in Durango, that surprised me."

Thinking about the event more, I suspect the guy was just trying to act tough to impress his friends. I guarantee the guy would have not made the comment if there were black people hanging out with us. And why did the comment upset me so much?

Comedian Dave Chappelle is one of the most hilarious and genius minds of my generation. Before disappearing out of the spotlight, he made two and a half seasons of *Chappelle's Show*, where he often made skits that covered racism in a comedic and unique way.

The most brilliant skit was "The Black White Supremacist," about a blind black man who was a leader in the white supremacist movement, able to hide his skin color under the guise of a KKK outfit. Blind and surrounded by racist white people, no one ever told him he was black. This skit was so genius because it nailed the absurdity of racism. Why does the color of one's skin matter? We may be of different hues, but we are all human.

I wondered why I was so upset about the racist remarks by a stranger, even if we did share some of the same friends. I started thinking back to my childhood, and realized there has always been a black person I've looked up to as a hero. As a child, it was Michael Jordan. When I grew into a man, it was Martin Luther King Jr. Learning about Dr. King and the civil rights era made me realize the importance of nonviolence and love. Today, I feel that many of our country's most brilliant minds are hip-hoppers, an art born in the black community. Hip-hop represents my generation and is the daily soundtrack to my existence. Black culture has always enriched my life and will continue to. I'm actually looking forward to being an old man, rolling up to some youngsters at a stoplight and bumping some 2Pac. God knows what the kids will be listening to then.

Last month, while working on the alumni magazine for my alma mater, Western State Colorado University, I interviewed a gentleman named Melvin Foote, who is the president of the Constituency for Africa, based in Washington, DC. Coincidentally, Foote, who is black, is from Rockford, Illinois, the same town where most of my family lives. Before moving to Colorado, he grew up poor and didn't even know a single college graduate prior to attending Western. After college, he joined the Peace Corps, went to Ethiopia, and has spent the rest of his life dedicated to helping the people of Africa. He's rubbed shoulders with many influential leaders, including Nelson Mandela and Colin Powell. I reached out to Melvin earlier this week while working on this piece to discuss racism.

Most of what we discussed I expected. Of course, we talked about slavery and how everything is tied back to that. Foote shared with me that racism is less direct now than it was in the '60s when he was in college and is now more institutional.

Then he talked about those younger than me. He spoke of his daughter, who is seventeen years old, and her group of friends, who are both white and black. "They don't judge each other by their skin color but rather the content of one's character," he said, quoting Dr. King. "They treat each other like sisters."

Then he talked about children even younger than her. "In a few years, there are going to be kids that are seven to eight years old that have never known anything other than a black president."

When he said that, it made me think of my own life, and what I've known and seen in my very short thirty-four years. I wasn't brought up in a racist environment, and that is probably why I am not racist. I was raised in a time where black people were not inferior, but were they were my peers, and my heroes. I didn't live through the civil rights movement of the '60s but rather the aftermath, the path toward equality for all human beings, and that is something to be proud of.

So, I think that's what pissed me off and shocked me the most, that someone could blatantly make racist comments in front of several people he did not know. In retrospect, though, forty or fifty years ago, it may have been commonplace for a white man to make such comments about black people. Today it is not. That alone is a small victory.

In closing, I wish I had a few thousand more words to reflect on this issue. There is a very similar struggle for equal rights going on for those who love the same sex. I can only hope my children grow up in a time where everyone who loves each other can get married and share their love openly, regardless of whether they are homosexual or heterosexual. After all, God is love.

And wishing I had more time, more words, I'll just leave you with a few that I first heard from a rapper, Andre 3000 of Outkast, "No one is free when others are oppressed."

This piece was originally published in the Durango Telegraph, *circa 2013.*

For the Sixties, for Hip-Hop

This one is for the sixties

This one is for hip-hop

These feelings I wear on my tank top

All day every day
I listen to hip-hop

And when I'm not
I'm chillin'
Like a villain
Listening to Bob Dylan

And always I show
These feelings on my tank top

I love hip-hop
But
I ain't hip-hop

No, fuck that wackness
I am hip-hop
You, me, we is hip-hop

Hip-hop was born from
Africa, New York, Jamaica
And the civil rights movement
A cause that was right
When black and white
Teamed up in peace

But Martin got killed
And so did the Kennedys
And Medgar Evers
And so many others

And everyone was over it

That peace

But black and white
And races of so many colors
Died so I could write
This.
So I gotta be ready to die
Like the B.I.G.
I gotta be a bigger Me
We all gotta be

No more white guilt for me
When you know you're not guilty
Cause white guilt
Just makes me feel guilty
And life goes by too quickly
To always be feeling guilty
Cause I know I'm on the right side
And the right side ain't that all white side

This one is for the sixties

This one is for hip-hop

"But I knew I was fly

When I was just a caterpillar

That I'd make it even if I didn't make a million"

—Chance the Rapper, "Everything's Good"

The Underwear Story, a Prelude

If you've been reading my stuff for a while now, you're probably aware of "The Underwear Story." Some of you probably think I'm a bit self indulgent, maybe something of a narcissist because of it.

I learned a while ago, a story is a story, and when it takes on a life of its own, you must sit back and think what your intentions were when you first wrote it. And with the underwear story, when I sought out my dream to become an underwear model for Patagonia, my intentions were to make a story, and a dream, out of a joke.

I won't bother with a full recap here, the original underwear story is in my first book, *Climbing Out of Bed*, and the second part follows this prelude, but I figured there was still more to the story that I wanted to provide.

When the original underwear story was published, my life was in shambles a bit. I was unemployed just after the 2008 recession. I was house-sitting for the month in a cabin in the woods, and I was terribly lonely. No job. No girlfriend. I was new to the town I was living in, Durango, and I was at that stage in life where I'd made so many big life changes, but I'd yet to see the results. I was hungry to be a writer, but I'd yet to publish a book. Walking into the local bookstore provided a significant amount of anxiety, because I knew I had no title to offer the readers, their eyes and hearts hungry for stories. I was hungry to tell my stories.

Around 2006, when I wrote the first draft of the underwear story, I e-mailed it to the Patagonia catalog to see if they would publish it. They didn't. But a few years later, blogs and social media blew up, and I resent the piece. They published it on their blog, and the story got a ton of reads. It began my professional relationship with Patagonia, a company that everyone in this industry wants to be connected with because of their values and their success. Timing is everything.

So that day when the story was first published, and I watched the likes, the comments, and the traffic, I realized that timing was everything. The Internet was really changing the world. And potentially my career. That day, a lot of people read it and thus formed an opinion about it, and about me. My joke had become something real.

That afternoon, after doing my thing in town in Durango, I drove back to the house-sitting gig (in reality it was a farm-sitting gig) and did my daily chores: I fed the pigs, the horses, the chickens, and finally, the cat.

Though I was secluded at this time, and had all the time in the world to write, I didn't really write. Writing is a funny thing—there's a unique recipe for productivity that is different for each and every writer. I was learning that excessive solitude was actually really bad for my writing. I prefer seclusion in the morning for my writing, but after that, I like to be around people for the rest of the day.

The following day, while online, I noticed my friend Shaun had started a petition. The petition read "Patagonia's Next Top Underwear Model," and I watched in amazement at how many people signed it. Shaun encouraged me to send it to my contact, Kasey, at Patagonia. I thought it was silly to do that. Shaun kept pushing, so I finally did.

Now at this time in life, I needed help. I had these dreams, but like many idealistic dreamers, I had no idea how to pair the dreams with business. That's where Shaun came in. He was just back in the mountains after several years working in marketing and event planning in various cities, culminating with a few years in New York City. I could write, but all the dreams were still seedlings. Shaun encouraged me to start putting numbers and desired outcomes onto paper. He had been successful in the business world but ultimately grew burned out on it and wanted "back in" to the lifestyle of living in a small mountain town. When we hung out, he would give me these elaborate pep talks. He made me believe in me. We all need that sooner or later. No human is an island. We can't do a damn thing on our own, at least not with elaborate schemes and dreams.

So, the publishing of the underwear story, in some weird way, gave me some optimism. My head was hanging pretty low during this era. I felt alone in a lot of ways. Sometimes it's good to have validation from the world, even it it's as weird as something like a joke to become an underwear model for Patagonia.

Something else to get out of the way is that I don't think I have the "look" of a male model. That's a weird sentence to write—I mean what straight male actually looks at other male models? We all know the "look" of a female model, all skinny and detached looking usually, but the only image of a male model that pops into my head is from *Zoolander*. Also, I don't feel like women check me out on a regular basis. Women are, of course, the greatest mystery. However, if I can rant, women do check me out when I'm wearing a tank top. Like a lot. So apparently, the best thing I have going on for me is that six inches of shoulder that a T-shirt covers up. Lesson learned, women like my shoulders, not my face.

But I'm not trying to sell my shoulders here; I'm trying to sell underwear, well at least photos of me wearing underwear.

Now at this point, I had virtually zero professional contacts in the business realm of the outdoor industry. I'd just started *The Climbing Zine*, and our ad content consisted of a few local shops and eateries. And then all of a sudden, my first real contact was with Patagonia! And all the result of the "underwear dream"!

The following day, I woke up and didn't write, again. I've never believed in writer's block, and this era was the ultimate test for that. There's a certain value to writing; everything in writing comes out of nowhere, from the ether, from God, whatever you want to call it. How it goes from being an idea to being recorded on the written page is a mystery, right up there with one of the greatest mysteries, like women. I guess art, music, and dance are all like that too, any creative thing. So there I was not believing in writer's block and experiencing writer's block.

Another weird coincidence happened exactly around the time the story was published: I lost my lucky red underwear. Like, one minute I had them, and the next minute they were gone. I was moving from house to house though, nearly every month for house-sitting gigs, and somehow they didn't survive the move to the "farm." I guess they served their purpose though, and soon after, Patagonia hooked me up with some freshies.

That next day, after the world read about me and my dream to become an underwear model, the most memorable thing that happened to me was that I chased a pig around the farm, running around in circles until I finally wrangled the beast back into its cage. I shoveled some horseshit into the corral. just to give him a little snack, and then fed the other animals. This house-sitting gig was full of all sorts of interesting memories; the following summer, I watched the place for the weekend and brought a date up there one evening. We milked the goats and gave the milk to a baby pig, which was cute, but you just knew he was going to grow up and eat shit and lay around in shit, just like all pigs do.

Eventually, and much to my chagrin, Kasey suggested I come out to Ventura to do a joke photo shoot at the Patagonia headquarters. As you'll see in the story that follows, that never panned out, but I did manage to connect with one of their photo editors in Yosemite, this really sweet woman named Jenning. We'd been playing phone tag, and the morning I was set to leave, I gave her a call, which went something like this.

"Hey, Jenning. It's Luke. I was just wondering if we could connect this morning. I'm getting ready to leave the valley."

"Oh, cool. That would be great…and, just so you know, I'm not really sure what's going on here…"

I thought that Kasey had filled her in on the joke, but she had no idea. I felt a tinge of fear that my dream might not happen, and all of a sudden the power of my dream lifted me to bravery, that even if I achieved nothing in my life, I would have once been an underwear model.

"Just meet me in the El Cap Meadow," I said. "I'll explain everything."

Years later, after I'd established myself more as a writer, I was working on ticking off all the magazines and podcasts I wanted on my byline, and near the top of the list was *The Dirtbag Diaries* podcast. I had several conversations with Becca Cahall, and we brainstormed all types of ideas. I even wrote up a three-thousand-word story about how climbing saved my life, something that ended up growing into my memoir, *American Climber*. Though she liked the story, she didn't feel that it fit with what she was looking for, so she passed on it. For the next few months, I kept brainstorming, but nothing really came to me. Becca was still supportive of my desire to be a part of *The Diaries* and told me she'd keep an eye on my stories.

Months later, I received an e-mail from Jen Altschul from *The Diaries* team. She had spent some time looking through various pieces I'd posted on the website for *The Climbing Zine*. Out of everything, she somehow found "The Underwear Story Part 2" and extended an invitation that I found quite amusing: "We'd like to work with you on that one and turn it into a piece for *The Diaries*."

And, in spite of myself, and all this other writing I was way more proud of, the underwear dream continued.

The Underwear Story Part 2, Dreams Coming True

When a dream is achieved, a new level of consciousness can be entered. During a recent road trip, full of California dreaming, I achieved two personal dreams: climbing El Capitan in Yosemite, and becoming an underwear model for Patagonia.

Both dreams were mere sparks at first. Any climber that sees El Capitan considers climbing it, if they could, and if they ever would. The first time I saw El Cap, I wanted to go home and forget about climbing—the mere sight of it revealed my most inner doubts and fears; at the same time, it was an object of beautiful desire, engaging and impossible to forget. Over the last decade plus, Yosemite's walls have allured me back time and time again, and after ten trips and two previous failures on El Cap, last September I finally climbed the Salathe Wall with my dear friend, Dave Ahrens.

It was the best-of-times kind of climb, with the perceived fear worse than the actual fear, and off-widths so humbling even the grade of 5.7 was intimidating. At one point, I found myself hanging on a #6 Camalot in a 5.7 pitch known as The Ear. I would nominate this pitch for consideration as "Hardest 5.7 on the Planet."

After succeeding on our lifetime goal, Dave and I had a couple of days in Yosemite to loiter and be thankful for the fruits of the horizontal. We participated in the Yosemite Facelift cleanup with our local homies, Mark Grundon and Scott Borden, and both agreed that picking up trash was probably the only thing we were capable of after the physical, emotional, and mental intensity of El Cap.

I may not be much of a climber, but I love it, and to have achieved that dream to climb El Cap left me in a state of contentment, almost. There was still one dream I wanted to realize in Yosemite—my dream to become an underwear model for Patagonia.

This dream, first suggested to me by my friend Amber Jeck, originally seemed just as improbable as climbing El Capitan. (For the full backstory read "The Underwear Story" in *Climbing Out of Bed*.) I mean, an underwear model is the king of all male models, right?

My dream seemed like a joke for years, a conversation piece at parties, something I thought I'd talk about forever, but never get to actually do. That all changed last year when Patagonia published the story about my underwear dream, which is an excerpt from my book, *Climbing Out of Bed*, on *The Cleanest Line*, their blog. Shortly after this my buddy Shaun Matusewicz started an online petition for me to fulfill my dream, which motivated me to write a formal request to Patagonia. To my delight, they thought I had what it takes to be an underwear model and agreed that I could indeed model their undies!

The only catch was that I needed to visit the Patagonia headquarters in Ventura, California, to do the shoot. I live in Durango, Colorado, a day's drive away from Ventura, so the dream was still somewhat improbable. Dreams are always improbable, impossible, or difficult though; improvisation would be necessary. Then it hit me, we could do the shoot during my upcoming trip to Yosemite, in the most iconic of all places for a photo shoot, the El Cap Meadow. I contacted my liaison at Patagonia, Kasey Kersnowski, to see what he thought of the idea. Always one to go out of his way to help me out, Kasey realized that some Patagonia employees would be in Yosemite at the same time for the Facelift.

It happened our last morning before leaving Yosemite. Dave and I met up with Jenning Steger, a photo editor for Patagonia. I explained to her my dream, and she was more than happy to take some time before climbing to do the shoot. We talked climbing for a bit, and then I stripped down to a new pair of Patagonia underwear. I was jacked on coffee, and the air had a brisk autumn coolness to it, but I managed to keep my swagger. I couldn't help but think about that Seinfeld episode where Kramer takes pictures of George in his underwear: with Kramer's voice in my head, "Give it to me. Work it. You're a man. You're a loverboy."

Then, lying down in the cool grass of the meadow, I did the pose I imagined underwear models do, with one hand on my hip and the other on my head, elbow stretched to the sky. I felt so at home in front of the camera, in the El Cap Meadow, that I realized, maybe I really do have a future in modeling. We talked climbing and photography some more with Jenning, and then we were on our way back to Colorado.

My dream was finally achieved; I did a real underwear-modeling shoot with Patagonia! The whole drive home we laughed about it. Then the cosmic coincidences continued.

My first day back at my day job, working at a Mexican restaurant, a customer grabbed my attention. I thought I'd done something wrong; after all, I knew my mind was still in Yosemite. She started off, "Now, I'm not trying to be weird or anything, but I used to work in the fashion industry...have you ever considered doing any modeling?"

Too surprised to really answer the question, I just stood there, jaw on the floor, wondering what else might be in store for me in my underwear.

This piece was originally published on Patagonia's blog, The Cleanest Line *(www.cleanestline.com)*.

Creeksgiving

No place soaks up sun like the Johnny Cat enclave at the Cat Wall, Indian Creek. The maroon cliffs are striped with perfect cleaved fissures, like vertical gateways into a hidden world. The desert heat can be oppressive, but in late autumn, the low golden rays cast long shadows over the walls.

We, the climbers—all smiles, scrapes, taped hands, and colorful costumes—are the gatekeepers against anything from the outside that might intrude. I'm reminded of Kerouac and his Beat Generation: they left behind the postwar clutter of new televisions, shiny cars, and urban sprawl to climb mountains and collect frost-white granite, blazing meteors, and volcanic ash in words. We, too, live simply, beaten by wind and by stone, trying to access something larger, something enclosed in the rocks and in ourselves.

We watch Mark climb that "thing to the right of Johnny Cat." Mark wears a black-and-gold cape that glitters in the sun. The crack is so narrow his fingers must feel as if they're being run over by an eighteen-wheeler.

He places tiny cams while the cape dangles and then flaps horizontally. This could be a movie. The maroon wall is the screen, and our superhero is engaged in a battle for good; the villain is gravity, or perhaps, doubt and fear. Our hero screams and jams and finds tiny edges for his feet. And then—*bam*!—he's flying off the rock. The crowd cheers. Another year of Creeksgiving is kicked off.

An acid test of sorts for the climbing community, this nonevent was born of friends gathering for Thanksgiving weekend at the Superbowl campsite in the early 2000s. There was a man they called the Mayor, a stubble-faced sage who took care of everyone with a slyly welcoming grin.

One year, it rains as it never does in the desert: continuously, filling up long-forgotten washes, and ensuring that the Wingate Sandstone is soaked for days.

Sure, we could start drinking, but instead we stage a 4K footrace around the campground. I pull a variety of costumes out of a duffel bag. Our friend Shaun works for an athletic company, and he produces a bag of socks and hats. That night, we have a dance off. People wrestle in the mud—grown men driven to madness by rain and alcohol, writhing on the desert floor.

"This is America's greatest footrace," Adam proclaims the next year. We run a half-marathon beneath a dark-blue sky, just a handful of us, one wearing a one-piece cat suit, another a Luigi costume. We jog from Superbowl to the distant ramparts of South Six Shooter Peak; we'll Jumar up it before running back.

Adam is a college friend from Gunnison, Colorado. When I met him, he was into ecstasy and raver parties. Then he grew up and sought adventure in other forms. He was once robbed at gunpoint in South Africa, and he told me, wide eyed, "It was so cool." He skis powder, floats rivers, loves women, and screams about "cutting the rope" *Vertical Limit* style at the climbing gym. His eyes are as blue and deep as glacial tarns. He's ready, at any moment, to erupt into maniacal laughter.

I follow his wild blond mane through a wash, silent, moving slowly. My feet sink into the fine pink grains; my breath guides me through sand and stone.

On the way back, we gaze at distant landmarks: North Six Shooter, the Cliffs of Insanity, the Happy Submarine. Six Shooter rises, proud and lean, like a crimson pistol. To our right is the Submarine; it has all the features of a sub, including a tiny periscope.

I fall behind. Adam carries on, his Jim Bridwell–inspired shirt glistening with psychedelic colors, and then he fades into the desert, disappearing behind a small hill.

That night at the Superbowl, the Mayor attends to the turkeys. He wears a big black moustache and devil's horns. While we were running, he spent the entire day cooking six turkeys in carefully excavated pits.

A group of sixty gathers around the fire, and each climber takes a turn stating what he or she is thankful for. At the dance off, a man in a pink suit ekes out a narrow victory over a man who strips down to his underwear and sprays everyone with cheap champagne. The liquid is sticky, a sugary dew upon our faces.

The following noon, thirty of us arrive at the Pistol Whipped wall. The bright greens and yellows of our outfits replace the long-ago-wilted desert flowers. Adam has to leave for Salt Lake City. He and his girlfriend, Amber, say the things that people who are leaving Indian Creek say: "Sorry we have to bail. I've got work tomorrow." "We'll see you soon, though—you're coming to Salt Lake this winter, right?" In front of them are the cracks and the secret world within the stone. Behind is the valley with its coruscations of sandstone running to the horizon, the dusty floor dotted with cottonwoods and red willows, silent with oncoming winter.

When the weather is good and the body is able, no one ever wants to leave. We've just met Amber, and she jokes about writing us letters. I love people who write letters, and I tell her so.

A month later while skiing, Adam dies in an avalanche. Thirty years old. I haven't known the death of a close friend until now, and part of him stays with me, a voice in my head. Sometimes, it's as if he's still there, standing in the iron-stained dust below the crag on that perfectly hungover long-ago Friday.

The next year Shaun builds a wooden structure he names Adam's Arch; adorned with prayer flags, it's the starting line for the races. By now, nearly all visitors to Indian Creek use the name Creeksgiving. The numbers swell in the Superbowl. Our dinner table is as long as Supercrack, with a hundred-person queue.

35

During dinner, we have Timmy Foulkes's Television, our imaginary TV station, with programming ranging from the telephone game to moustache competitions. Revelers wear rabbit costumes; there is a man with a horse head, a woman in a skintight fishnet top and black pleather pants. And there is pink, lots of pink—a pink wig, pink tights—and gold, so much gold.

Sixty people pass a strip of LED lighting across our checkered linoleum dance floor. We dance until the stars fade into alpenglow.

Creeksgiving has grown too big. We know it. Apparently, so do the authorities. The following spring at Creekster (a knock-off minicelebration during Easter), we catch the Utah police spying from the bushes. We decide to have fun with them and stage a silent moustache competition. I imagine those officers back at the station: "Well, Sarge, we tried to bust those hooligans, but they were actually really quiet. They did hold a moustache competition though."

And then, just like that, our Creeksgiving is over. We don't gather at the Superbowl the following year. We're all getting older. We've cried enough tears of joy at weddings to make an arroyo flow. We're less committed to living like dirtbags and more committed to something else. You could call it love. Or life. Or adulthood. The word *Creeksgiving*, however, remains part of the lexicon, and climbers still gather under its name. Every autumn, I see the forum posts: "Who's going to Creeksgiving this year?"

I was fortunate to partake in this absurd celebration when climbers with wigs took whimsical whippers, and we danced as if no one were watching. Creeksgiving was our own little Golden age, encapsulated in magic and reverie, a point in time when, if a man in a golden cape had simply taken flight into the heavens or disappeared into the rock, I wouldn't have been surprised.

It never occurred to me that those moments could simply vanish, or that any one of us could. We never do; if we're living right, we simply live, in the moment.

I wish I could say I hold on to some ideal parting image of Adam—say, at that perfect instant atop a sandstone tower, where the afterburn of adventure blends with the camaraderie of partnership. Instead, I recall blurry fragments. Adam's house in Salt Lake City days after his death, filled with his paperback books, skis, bikes, and one lone flower, still blooming and cared for by his roommates. His lucky piece, the pink Tri-Cam, which we barely discovered in a snow patch in front of his house. His quiet voice uttering the best piece of advice he ever gave me, "Just breathe." And the time at the Creek when Adam and I sat on a tailgate and saw a shooting star blaze across the sky. In an instant, the object was gone, but countless other stars dotted the heavens. We sat there, breathing, dreaming, drifting off toward sleep.

"Wouldn't it be crazy to witness a comet hit the Earth and destroy us all?" I asked.

All Adam said was, "That would be so awesome!"

I know that in whatever incarnation future Creeksgivings will take, Adam will be there—closest to us when we're scraping up some sandstone crack that cuts deep into raw skin or running through a desert wash draped in psychedelic hues or gathering with our faces lit by firelight—a spirit made of stardust, illuminating our bacchanal from the proscenium arch of the heavens.

This piece was originally published in Alpinist, *Issue 48.*

I don't really feel it's right to conceal your pain

it bubbles up inside and people start killing things

—Collective Efforts, "Let It Alone"

Vulnerability

Did you know?

2016 is the year of vulnerability?
That no matter what
It's cool to be the real you
And the real me
That's vulnerability

No more: frontin-fakin-takin
from your real self
it's time for feeling-loving-opening
To your real self

Cause we're fucking tired of
your Facebook self
your selfie self
your real self
is what we crave

Tell your selfie stick
It can suck my ----

Lick.

That envelope
and write yourself a letter
tell yourself your heart wants better

Vulnerability.
I'll look at me.
And realize I ain't as cool
As I said I was last year
Or even that last beer

This year
I'll write with tears
I'll be unafraid
of my beating heart
Telling my brain to
Listen to that pain

The space between the heart and the brain
Imagine the possibility
Imagine the vulnerability

It ain't 2004 no more though
It's 2016, all fresh and so clean

The cool you is the real you
You know that Andre 3000 you
the cool you is the real you
even if it's the you who thinks that
Ja Rule is still cool you

We all want to see it
Let that mutherfucker go
You can do it slow
or fast

Let that open-hearted you
do some writing
or some poetry reciting
We wouldn't all be here tonight
if the possibility of real
wasn't so exciting

so inviting
so enlightening

Everyone wants that real you
That always says something true you
That walking with the swagger
of zero ego you

That you anyone can talk to

That vulnerable you

That's the you I want to be introduced to.

Graduating from College Me

I awoke in the Indian Creek desert to the sound of a crying baby. I tossed and turned over in the back of my Subaru—it's always a good morning when I wake up in the back of my car—and sat there basking in a new sort of nostalgia. The tribe is growing.

Our tribe, those who believe and know our outdoor experiences define who we are and shape our existences, is constantly ebbing and flowing. New friends and kindred spirits are essential to recreation, but with Persephone, the crying baby, well, she is truly the first in my circle of friends to be brought this closely into the climbing world.

Sure, I have other friends who have kids, but most of them procreate and then seem to disappear off the face of the Earth. They move to places like Denver, Oklahoma, and Texas, and then they become the friends I talk to once a year on the phone. There's no fault in that; raising children is hard work, and I understand why many of my friends have left Colorado mountain towns for steady paychecks and domestication in the flatlands.

But Persie, her parents have stayed put, for now anyways, in Gunnison, and are still dedicated to climbing and skiing and all that comes with that lifestyle. This little sweetheart, she puts a tear in my eye and a smile on my face just thinking about her. So, to say the least, I didn't mind her crying that cold late-November morning. I couldn't have been happier to have her there.

In college, when I knew everything, I proclaimed to my parents that I was never having kids. I was sure of it. "There's already too many people on this planet," I told them. "Overpopulation is the number one environmental problem, so why should I contribute to that?"

When I shared this bit of information with a lady friend of mine in college, she replied, "You're going to be a lonely old man."

I replied with silence.

I know I'm a failure in the eyes of College Me. Everything was about the outdoors and the environment, and my professors seemed to plead to me—it is up to you to do something. I thought our generation was going to save the planet, and I thought I would be able to curb my consumption and carbon footprint. I envisioned myself driving a car that ran on hemp oil or hydrogen or something, living somewhere in a yurt where I raised and grew my own food, and writing ferociously like Edward Abbey, taking down the machine one sentence at a time.

And where am I? Ten years out of college and my Subaru is gulping down cheap gas like there's no tomorrow. My phone does really cool things, I buy most of my food at the grocery store, and my energy comes from all traditional sources that are contributing to climate change. At least weed is legal though—College Me has got to be stoked about that!

I don't have kids but not for environmental reasons; that notion has long faded. My belief now is that the outdoor-minded/liberal arts–educated folks are the ones that *should* be procreating. Saving the planet—impossible. Saving yourself and changing your ways—difficult, not impossible though.

The one thing I am proud of is knowing and appreciating the moment. Lose a friend to an avalanche, a motorcycle wreck, or a climbing accident and the truth is revealed: your time here is precious, and you are just a one-minute part of a complex world. Have you done something you're proud of? Are you doing at least one thing to put your life in the right direction? Is there someone still around that you really love? Yeah, you may not have grown up to be whom you wanted to be, but is there something that still gives you hope? Then that's what you live for. At least, that's what I live for. Hope. Friends. Love. The moment.

I don't have kids simply because I haven't met my life partner yet, and with a huge dash of good luck and proper usage of birth control. I know most women want kids, and I know there's nothing I love more than women, so College Me loses this argument. Seeing the changes that happen in women from their early twenties to late twenties has been eye opening as well—that biological clock thing they tell you about that never seems real until you witness it firsthand.

I think most single people who are grown adults have that one who got away. Or, maybe more than one. I can fondly reflect on a few. The other day on the phone, I was talking with a former lover who I once thought was The One Who Got Away. Eventually, I realized she wasn't, but she is still someone I highly respect and try to stay in touch with. She is also about to deliver her first baby. Educated, passionate, beautiful, and environmentally minded, she's going to be a great mother.

Our conversation wasn't overly profound. It revolved around what so-and-so is doing and how our careers are going, but I noticed she was eerily calm and centered. When we dated, she was in her midtwenties and certain she didn't want a child, but as she grew older and fell in love again, she realized for sure that she did want a kid. And so, she is having one.

As our conversation grew to a close, she said something that stuck with me. "You know, for most of our lives we're preparing to arrive. We're kind of always in that process of arriving at something."

Last week, I ventured out to Indian Creek to that same campground where we spent Thanksgiving; I was supposed to meet a friend, but I couldn't find her. The campground, which was full over the Thanksgiving holiday, was quiet, with not a single person in sight. I couldn't bear to stay; it was just too silent, and in that moment, my comfortable bed back home lured me away from a lonely, cold campsite.

So, I turned my Subaru around and headed back to Durango, looking forward to future days in the desert, surrounded by friends and little ones running around—a picture of the future College Me could have never imagined, one more beautiful than I ever could have dreamed.

This piece was originally published in the Durango Telegraph.

Last Thoughts on the Dirtbag

You know for me it all began looking
Looking for something real in this world

In the nineties
At the time "keep it real" was the phrase
We are talking like "back in the days"

Looking for Something
I could not find trapped in walls
So I started searching
Started climbing walls

Then I was depressed
And dreaming of the sixties
Like something was missing
I wanted Jack Kerouac
I wanted to bring him back
And I wanted to just pack up a rucksack
And never ever-ever-ever-ever look back

And something was missing
And Kerouac was long dead
And so was the Grateful Dead

But it wasn't time related
Really everything is related
And the only time we have is now

So I picked up a pen
Nothing,
Again and again
Like always before
'Cause I had no story to tell, yet
No story to sell, yet

So I picked up a pipe

And I picked up smoking
And I started choking
Something was missing

In the midst of all the dope
I picked up a rope
I picked up some hope

Because, my friends
It's either have heroes or have heroin
And the sharp end
Is better than the needle
But we all just want to feel

But
The rope was dangerous
And hope was dangerous

But it's good to be dope
And even to live a life
Even to be born
Into this world
Is dangerous

So here we are
And there we were

Doing it for the glory
Naw
Doing it for the story
Naw
Doing it for the poetry
Yeah

We were just two dope boyz
In a Cadillac
Rather that
We were two dope boyz
In a Subaru hatchback
Way before hashtags

When we didn't even know we were dirtbags
It was good to be a dirtbag

It was good to see
Sea to shining sea
Good to see America
Is not all just malls, cars, prisons, churches, and bars

Good to see there's some heroes left
Because all the heroes went left
Because you know it all started after I left
My past behind
So I could rewrite my future

Still no matter where you go
You are what you are

I wanted to write
I wanted to sink
Into the paper
Like I was ink
When I'm climbing, I'm trapped within the climb
I escape when I finish the line

I wanted to write something inspired by the sky, the rocks
Like you know forgetting about grades and clocks
And finding men and women who climb rocks

With all respects to the homie Jay Z
I gotta tell you the truth, B
It was not an empire state of mind
I was in a dirtbag state of mind

You know, because I learned
I could dig poetry
I could dig rappin'
I could dig scrappin'

I could dig jammin'
Hands, fingers, and feet

Whatever it took to make ends meet

Every day begun
With the sun
And retired
With the fire

Looking for hope over every bend
Hoping each and every day would never end
Never ending feeling of climbing, so Zen
So Zen, we had to do it, again and again

It took us everywhere,
From J-Tree to Yosemite
From Devils Lake To Devils Tower
Smith Rocks to random rocks
We forgot about

But it always took us back to this desert

Of

Red Rocks
No clocks
Blue sky
No lie
Only the truth of pain, grits, and guts
Showing themselves in pride, and cuts

Red dirt on everything you own
Red dirt in everything you own

No suit and tie shit
Just climbing it

And forgetting what you looked like
Forgetting that this world just ain't right

Ed Abbey

48

He was gone too
But in our hearts
Desert Solitaire was like dessert, for the soul
The desert is for the soul

The Colorado Plateau
Like rock 'n' roll
Like hip-hop
We wouldn't stop
Oh hell no

We soon found we were carriers of a torch
Those who are too mad
Too beat, to be sad
All the time
All the rhymes
Wrote themselves

Living in poetry
Living like this life was meant to be
My friends
Because it is

It's about that hope you have
And that feeling like dope you have

So where do you look for this hope that you're seeking?
Where do find that campfire that's a burnin'
That will light your life for the rest of its days?

You can either look to the church of your choice
Or you can look for Bob Dylan in his golden days
Either way, you'll find them both in Indian Creek at sundown

This poem is also featured in the short film of the same name by Greg Cairns and Mehall. It can be found on Vimeo and YouTube.

The Memorial Toilet

A memorial toilet is a hard thing to explain.

But that's exactly what my friends were constructing last weekend, a new toilet in the Superbowl Campground in Indian Creek, Utah, to honor a fallen comrade, Kevin "K-Bone" Volkening, who died doing what he loved: climbing.

It all made sense to me; I'd heard about the project months beforehand. The campground where the toilet was placed gets a ton of traffic and only had one toilet for everyone to use. I've personally stood there while nature calls, behind a lengthy line of others who are heeding that same call. But when I try to explain the memorial toilet to others, it always comes out strange.

Me: "Yeah, it's a toilet they are building as a tribute to a friend of ours that passed away."

Random person: "So, they are honoring his life by building a toilet?"

See what I mean?

I've been traversing the land between Durango and Moab so many times this fall that, to the casual observer, I surely appear obsessed, inflicted with a healthy dose of masochism. Climbing the unforgiving red rock Wingate Sandstone cracks was number one on my agenda for October, aka Rocktober, and I've given that pursuit priority over everything else in my life. The only thing I've probably done more than climbing in Utah last month was my other passion: sleeping. God, do I love to sleep. And while we're making lists: women, I love women. Throw some food, water, and a forty-plus-hour workweek into that equation and that's my life. Happy, like that catchy gets-stuck-in-your-head-when-you-don't-want-it-to Pharrell song.

Anywho, while content as a pig in shit most of the time, I am not without my own demons and doubts. As a failed environmentalist and former Catholic, you can only imagine the guilt that I feel, even in the most day-to-day activities. I feel guilty that I'm burning through fossil fuels like it's my job just so I can merely recreate. There are rocks right here in Durango that I could climb. And why am I so obsessed with these particular rocks in Utah? Shouldn't I be doing something more meaningful with my life?

But, save for some moments in a lover's embrace, nothing feels more rewarding than climbing these rocks. And, it does put food on the table; I have the luxury of writing about my experiences, and occasionally getting a paycheck for it. So, I continue on.

And, I do feel like there's more of an exchange than mere physical gratification. I feel a connection with my creator out there. I love the joy of letting my mind become meditative and not sending fifty text messages, a hundred e-mails, and checking my Facebook thirty times a day. Perhaps I am afraid of becoming a machine, so I must go where I am a man again, where I must rely on my inner strength and survival instincts.

And, if I can dare go deeper, and quote the climbing legend Royal Robbins, who is to say that climbing isn't a search for God? We, lovers of nature, hold the wild lands of the Earth near and dear to our hearts, and would not want to live life without them.

But, wait, this is supposed to be an article about a toilet, and I'm writing about God? Back on track, let's go to Castle Valley, the day before the toilet was installed.

If Indian Creek is like living in a painting, Castle Valley is the masterpiece. Castleton Tower, the first in seven iconic summits on a ridgeline, is a perfectly square castle of sandstone, which stands so prominently that it is a natural lightning rod. The other towers and buttresses, given names such as The Rectory, The Priest, and The Nuns, suggest that the place is a spiritual haven, and in this environment, it's impossible not to feel inspired. As a side note, this area has seen more than one television stunt: Bon Jovi made the music video to "Blaze of Glory" on the summit of The Rectory and more

51

than one car company has helicoptered vehicles to the top of Castleton for commercials. (Search 1964 Chevrolet, Castleton Tower on YouTube and you won't be disappointed.)

So my buddy Dave and I are in Castle Valley, for Halloween, because I didn't want to party on Halloween this year, and we're climbing towers. Dave is one of my favorite climbing partners because he's mellow, safe, and smart. He's also getting married, and he just bought a house and got a cat, and well, I know these signs; I have to climb with him when he has the time, because he's just going to get busier and busier with life. The call from my climbing partners saying that they are either getting married or having kids is getting to be quite routine these days.

After climbing our first tower, The Rectory, I hunger for more. Dave seems content. I feel like a puppy dog that just has to be ran a little bit more, or that energy is going to get him in trouble. And, we begin a negotiation of sorts. "Well, I want to keep the fiancé happy. I shouldn't get back too late," he says.

"You can blame it on me," I suggest. "Throw me under the bus. I don't care."

"That's not how it works, bro," Dave says knowingly.

I play my cards carefully. "Well, how about we just do the first pitch." (Kinda like the climbing version of "just the tip.")

And somehow he agrees. We climb Castleton, and then I'm happy, and so is Dave, and we are standing on a beautiful summit, with views of Arches, the La Sal mountains, and even a peek into Colorado on the horizon. Stunning. We rappel off the tower, and then I have to make a decision: to drive back to Durango that night or roll down to Indian Creek and hang out with the crew that is installing the memorial toilet that weekend. I've got to be in Durango for work the following afternoon, so I don't have time to actually lend a hand, but I want to hang out with everyone and show my support.

Indian Creek wins. A campfire with many new faces, and it's that same ritualistic, timeless desert fire, while flash lightning illuminates the night. K-Bone's spirit is felt, as new friends meet and old ones unite. His infectious, friendly personality made K-Bone an instant friend for countless people.

In the morning, I meet Kolin Powick, who helped spearhead the project. Powick was able to put the memorial toilet into words better than I was, in my stumbling explanations.

"The goal was to create something long-lasting in K-Bone's name and honor at his most favorite climbing area on Earth," he later wrote. "We ended up with one of the most unique and special outhouses anyone could have imagined."

And they did. With over forty volunteers, including his Kevin's wife, Marge, his mother, his sister, and his brother-in-law, the toilet was constructed in about four hours.

I can't wait to sit on the throne.

This piece was originally published in the Durango Telegraph.

Lawton's Wall

Again, this one starts with a crying baby. This time the baby is Isabella, and we're deep in a wild Mexican canyon called El Salto, an hour from cell service, fifteen minutes from a village where people don't even have landlines or interwebs. Paradise.

I'm watching her sleep, pondering her preciousness and the delicate nature of humanity, while Dad is a hundred feet off the ground, pinching onto a limestone tufa, perfectly positioned on the orange-and-gray wall, while Mom belays, tending the rope to her husband.

Then, the baby wakes up and starts bawling. "Mama, mama, mama…"

I pick her up awkwardly and bring her closer to Mom. Dad finishes his route and is lowered down. Mom takes him off belay and gives the baby what it wants: milk. This routine was played out over and over again during a recent trip to the Monterrey region of Mexico, where my dear friends Mark and Norma live in the winter.

I write trip because I don't like the term vacation. I don't like to vacate when I travel—I like to experience, to be fully present, to feel it, to be inspired and moved, so I have something to write about when I return. The world can keep its fancy cruises and five-star hotels; let me sleep in the dirt and get sunburned and scraped by cactuses and beaten down by the wild, in order to feel something more

But let me back up. The plane ride. Falling in love with words again. I love reading, and that's the reason I'm a writer. All the truths are in books, and stories weave the fabric that is humanity. To have that opportunity myself to be on the creation end of storytelling is humbling; when someone tells me I've inspired them, it's the ultimate form of payment.

I'm falling in love on the plane, with *The Fault in Our Stars*. I don't read as much as I'd like because it's difficult to carve out time to read in the day-to-day grind of life. I've had *The Fault* sitting on my bookshelf for nine months, and I guess I picked it up at the right time because the story immediately creates that feeling that good writing creates: confirming the notion that life is short and precious. Plus, I'm a sucker for prose and poetry, and *The Fault* has just a perfect dose of that while it tells the sad story of young cancer patients on death's door.

In *The Fault*, there's this character the young cancer-stricken narrator refers to as "The Ball-less Wonder." He's a one-dimensional testicular-cancer survivor who leads a support group that the narrator reluctantly attends throughout the book. Right away, my thoughts lead to one question: *'Can you still have a sex drive without testicles?* I mean, sex is an important part of life, and I can't imagine a life without sex drive.

"Hormones," Mark starts with. Mark himself is a testicular-cancer survivor, who lost one of his testicles to cancer. "You have to take hormones if you lose both of your testicles."

Mark was never quite sure if his "boys could swim" postsurgery and had some sperm frozen before the removing of his testicle in case he ever wanted to father a child. Turns out, as evidenced by Isabella being in the world, his boys could indeed swim, and he didn't have to make a withdrawal from the sperm bank.

Mark got cancer in college, ten years ago, and to see him as a dad and husband makes me really happy. We share a hunger and passion for climbing, a feeling that we're always chasing, and for eight days he showed me the immense opportunities for climbing, mostly with the family along for the ride.

Our most memorable day of climbing was attempting a route called Lawton's Route, farther up the canyon in El Salto. It was just the boys this time; this was no place for babies. Our third companion was Joel, a Mexican dirtbag, fluent in English, a guy who is fighting for climbing access in another nearby canyon full of limestone and tufas. Monterrey is surrounded by limestone, with as much rock, maybe more, than the Moab desert.

The Monterrey area has had a wet and cold winter, abnormal weather everyone said. Because of this, we had to navigate a small, chilly, crystal-blue pool at the bottom of a cascading and winding waterfall. We debated for days how we were going to get our gear and ourselves across the pool, which ended up being about five feet deep. After a failed attempt for find a little raft at Walmart, Mark remembered his surfboards at the last minute.

The plan works well; we ferry our packs across on the surfboards and wade into the shoulder-deep water. It's chilly and wakes us up and gives us a feeling of adventure. After a half hour of those shenanigans and another twenty minutes of hiking, we arrive at the base of Lawton's Route.

Lawton's Route is named for my closest friend that has ever died, Adam Lawton. He was a skier, climber, boater, runner, and biker who had an insatiable appetite for adventure. He was killed in an avalanche in 2012, and Mark decided to bolt this four-pitch route in his memory. Mark successfully climbed the route after bolting it, and for the last three years, it has remained in obscurity.

A small plaque scratched on a tiny limestone rock marks the start of the climb, and I get all nostalgic and teary eyed thinking that deep in some Mexican canyon is a tribute for one of the finest human beings I ever knew. I can see his crooked, scheming smile in my mind.

Right after I smile because of his smile, we hear nearby rockfall, and I'm quickly snapped back to the moment.

"Can I lead the crux pitch?" I beg my friends.

They quickly agree. Mark leads the first part, grunting and occasionally cursing his way up it. "Dammit, Three-Years-Ago Mark," he jokes. "You should have placed more bolts."

When it's my turn to follow the pitch, ten feet up, I break off a hold, and with rope stretch, I fall about a foot from the ground. I also curse Three-Years-Ago Mark, but I get back on the rock and climb to the belay.

Then it's my turn to lead the second crux pitch. I pause briefly to take stock of my surroundings: palm trees grow from the rock; millions of cactuses do too; the river weaves drunkenly through the canyon; and behind us is an unclimbed thousand-foot wall, with a massive orange overhang; over the overhang is hundreds of feet of gray rock, soaring to the sky. It's like a Mexican-limestone-virgin version of Yosemite.

Fifty feet up, I'm scared, again cursing Three-Years-Ago Mark, yelling expletives to the rock. I try to channel Adam's spirit. Nothing. I think of Tommy Caldwell, the Dawn Wall hero, whom I share the exact same stats: 36 years old, 5´9˝, 150 pounds, lives in Colorado. Nothing. For every Caldwell there are ten thousand Mehalls: everyday climbers all too in tune with their lack of courage.

I hang on bolts, and finally, not gracefully, get to the next belay, painfully aware of my fragility, but somehow, none of the mistakes and cursing adds up to any sort of shame or failure. Climbing is a Zen sport, not a sport where we keep score.

The canyon is still beautiful; shortly, I'll be joined at this perch by one old friend and one new friend. And then, again, I smile and take stock of my surroundings.

This piece was originally published in the Durango Telegraph.

To Live Is to Fly

As I start this piece, it's that time of the year when the Animas River in Durango looks like a chocolate milkshake, and we're all shedding our clothes and living closer to the sun (and the rain).

I'm enjoying this weird spring weather. Sure, it gets in the way of our outdoor endeavors, but we need it, and the land needs it. Plus, to have snow-covered mountains this time of the year is really special. Big props to you hardcore skiers who are still getting after it; I hope the redemption feels divine. You deserve it.

Last week, the outdoor adventure community lost a major pillar in the form of BASE jumper and climber Dean Potter. When I started climbing in the late nineties, Dean was a climbing god. He would climb without a rope on El Capitan in Yosemite, thousands of feet above the ground and later invented a form of climbing that combined BASE jumping with free soloing, called FreeBASE, and he applied that on a notoriously difficult and dangerous wall, the Eiger in Switzerland. He was a dirtbag rebel, who only had one peer in climbing, Alex Honnold. With FreeBASE, he didn't have a peer; he was a lone bird flying through the skies of innovation, living closer to ecstasy, and death, than any of us could possibly imagine.

I felt fortunate to learn of Dean's passing by word of mouth. I really hate finding out about death through a computer screen, even if it's not someone I know personally. I'd spent the afternoon with my ladyfriend and was getting ready to head over to a barbeque. She was checking her laptop and told me, "Dean Potter died," followed by, "BASE jumping."

The words echoed in my head. It wasn't a surprise. Dean had been using up his nine lives over and over again, and even if he seemed like a god, he was indeed a human. He died with another fellow BASE jumper, Graham Hunt, in Yosemite, in quick succession, crashing into a wall below a notch they'd hoped to clear.

I put my head down and let the death sink in. Then I smoked one for Dean.

58

BASE jumping makes other risky sports look like golf; the risk is so high that I don't think anyone can be truly surprised when a BASE jumper dies. That does, however, do nothing to lessen the sadness for their loved ones. I felt sad to see how quick some people were to judge their risk taking in various online forums and editorial columns. I followed Dean's pursuits for years, and he made it clear that his dreams were to fly. He wrote about his dreams and nightmares and felt a deep calling to fly. And so he did. And he flew until he couldn't anymore. And, maybe he's reincarnated into a flying creature now, above us with only a distant memory of his past life. I'm not a religious man, but such energy does not seem like it would die.

I met Dean a couple times but was unable to ever get past the fanboy stage in conversation. That was a shame because Dean was always fully present and didn't seem to think he was better than me. The best memory I have of Dean, though, is a time when we were both climbing on the walls of Yosemite.

My friend Dave and I were slow at work on the Washington Column, a beginner big wall that many climbers use as their first long Yosemite wall climb. It was mid-November, and we toiled away for a couple days and came away with sweet victory, even sweeter because a big storm rolled in that night and closed the autumn climbing season for good. The next day, we learned that Dean and his friend Sean Leary had climbed The Nose on El Capitan in just over two and a half hours, which at the time was the record. In the time that we climbed one hundred feet, they raced up nearly three thousand feet on El Cap.

Sadly, Leary died BASE jumping last year, and Potter had to go search for his body. I still feel deeply inspired by their athletic feats and sad for their friends and family that they are no longer with us as humans.

To judge their risks, as many have done, seems to be a cheap shot to the lives they led and the loved ones they left behind. Their deaths are a reminder that this thing we call life is a miracle, an unexplained phenomenon of living and breathing that is so incredibly fantastic at times we should stop to consider the vastness of it. That we should pour all our energy into loving each other, because when we're done, that's really all any of us are going to be remembered for.

59

Lately, I've been blessed and encouraged to follow my own dreams, and I've been planning lots of trips that, God willing, I'll be able to write about and pay for my travels with what I earn from the stories. Last month, my friend Shaun and I decided we would travel to Yosemite together, again. We've had many failures there on El Capitan and other walls, and we want to go back for redemption. We agreed that we should try The Nose, often called "the best rock climb in the world."

The next day, after Shaun and I decided we were going to try The Nose, I got a text from my friend Eric about the death of a young climber on The Nose. I soon learned that it was Tyler Gordon, a Durango local, who recently graduated from the University of Colorado in Boulder. He was high on The Nose when he fell two hundred feet to his death, after he'd failed to clip in properly. I didn't know Tyler, but I can guess some of you reading this are still mourning him. What else can I write other than my thoughts and prayers are with you.

Despite the inherent risk of climbing, Shaun and I will still travel to Yosemite in September to touch the magical stone that is El Cap. In the face of the deaths of close ones and heroes, I used to ponder if the risks we take in our outdoor pursuits were worth it. I've answered that question with a resounding yes, many times over. I have other questions to God that I suppose will only be answered when I reach my own death. Until then, those that have passed will know, and I'll try to move delicately and carefully, with those who have passed living right next to where my heart beats.

This piece was originally published in the Durango Telegraph.

Stack that Cheese, Becoming a Hip-Hop Historian

"Luke, what does *smack that cheese* mean?" two of my college-aged co-workers asked me the other day.

We were closing down the restaurant, and like usual, we were listening to hip-hop. The subject matter of the question: a song by Lupe Fiasco, in which the chorus is "stack that cheese."

"It's not 'smack that cheese,'" I explained to the ladies. "It's 'stack that cheese.' Cheese is money, and to stack money means to save it, stash it away."

Another piece of the modern lexicon was added to their brilliant young minds, and we went back to cleaning. Then I wondered, *When did I become a hip-hop historian?*

For me, hip-hop is a love-hate relationship. If there is one form of music that speaks directly to my heart, it is hip-hop. If there is one form of music that disgusts me, it is hip-hop. Hip-hop is alive. Hip-hop is dead. Hip-hop is sitting on the mountaintop, singing the praises and joys of being alive. Hip-hop is down in the gutter, sipping hard liquor and syrup, waiting to be resurrected. Hip-hop is a reflection of the human condition.

I don't remember where my first hip-hop tape came from, probably a Sam Goody store at the mall, but I remember its manila color and the energetic vibes that the Beastie Boys created. It was *Licensed to Ill*, a 1980s classic, with Led Zeppelin–sampled guitar riffs and outrageous lyrics. Lyrics that would later shape high school and the excessive partying that led into higher education. Simply put, the Beastie Boys were trouble, and what does the confused youth love more than trouble?

In high school, when the world moved into CDs, I kept Snoop Dogg and Dr. Dre stashed away in my desk, for fear my parents would find them. In essence, the songs on *Doggystyle* were similar to *Licensed to Ill*: partying, misogyny, and standard misbehaving, which is exactly what I wanted to get into as a teenager.

I now look back to the 1990s with nostalgia. So out of reach. Many say the golden age of hip-hop was in the 1990s. In the nineties, to me, hip-hop was simply rap, music that was made for partying, for escape, firmly removed from reality. In my senior year of hip-hop, I decided I was tired of rap and became a hippie, perhaps just for a change in drugs to do at parties.

So the golden age of hip-hop, a crescending wave, crashed over before I even realized it was there. Luckily, at my third college, up in Gunnison, Colorado, I realized there was more to live for than partying. There was the outdoors.

Hip-hop was invented in the concrete streets, in New York in the 1970s. Founded within black culture, there were three essential ingredients in hip-hop: music, graffiti art, and break dancing. It didn't take long for hip-hop to spread across the globe, or to become commercialized. Still, today, the essence of hip-hop remains alive and vibrant: kids are still rapping, dancing, and creating art with the same tools from the inventors (at least in a figurative sense) from America to Zimbabwe.

So I moved from an urban existence in Illinois to the rural Rocky Mountains of Colorado and finally discovered the true beauty and genius of hip-hop. I made the transition from being a hippie, to being, well, just me. Doors began to open in my mind. My friends and I would take trips all over the country to climb, and hip-hop was always on the stereo.

One buddy in particular, Bennett Powell, aka Big Red the Superjock, was a DJ on the local radio station in Crested Butte, and we had intricate discussions about our favorite artists and their work. Hip-hop was more than just music for partying, way more.

Hip-hop is art; it is about knowledge and self-discovery, and in the words of my second favorite duo, Black Star, "That life without knowledge is, death in disguise? That's why, knowledge of self is like life after death. Apply it, to your life, let destiny manifest."

I learned about the drug epidemic, about how many rappers only escaped jail because they got into hip-hop (former crack dealer Jay Z being the most famous). The anger and injustice of four hundred years of slavery was voiced through many artists. Tough and honest voices against capitalism, though, hip-hop has been noted as the only procapitalist form of music out there (again, the contradictions). Another great duo, dead prez, raps about a proper diet, exercise, love, poetry, and yoga: "They say you are what you eat, so I strive to eat healthy, my goal in life is not to be rich or wealthy."

My favorite was (is) Andre 3000, of the duo Outkast. Such a poetic pure soul, Andre 3000 is still ahead of his time, twenty years into his career. He embraced the cool of hip-hop, while remaining true to himself: "Softly as if I play piano in the dark, found a way to channel my anger not to embark. The world's a stage and everybody's got to play their part."

When Andre 3000 raps, whether it is about struggle, drugs, violence, or love, you feel his soul. When he says, "we the coolest mutherfunkers on the planet," you *feel* like the coolest mutherfunker on the planet.

Even the Beastie Boys came around. My path mirrored theirs. After years of partying and debauchery, they started rapping about meaningful topics. They apologized for their misogyny and stopped carrying weapons. They started getting involved in the Free Tibet movement and featured Buddhist monks on one of their tracks. Before his untimely death, Adam Yauch, aka MCA, spent a winter dirtbagging it as a snowboarder at Alta Ski Area.

So there it is, a brief history of how I became a hip-hop historian. I kinda like it that, like myself, hip-hop has a few gray hairs. The art is getting better, and worse, all at the same time. It's everywhere, from commercials to street corners, but the essence of hip-hop lies within the doers: the graffiti artists, the break-dancers, the up-and-coming rappers, people trying to make something from nothing.

And if you're still confused whether you should be smackin' or stackin' your cheese, you can buy me a beer; we'll talk.

This piece was originally published in the Durango Telegraph, *circa 2014.*

Squamish Summer

Blackberry bushes beneath
Golden Granite

Days planned
Rarely do they go
According to plan

Slabs say trust me
But don't trust me
Trust yourself

Filling our futures with follies and fantasies
Knowing there will be falls on walls
Whippers runouts fear and failure
And being okay with it

Climbing is my daily bread
Like water it keeps me going
Keeps the mind sharp
The muscles moving
But, why? Why?
Have I given so much to it?

Squamish steals my heart
Where the granite meets the sea
I see myself for many summers
But you can only have one summer
At a time

Fit women wander with wanderlust
I wonder what women will meet my lust next
I've been blessed to have so many
Alas, I only want one

I gotta keep pushing and striving
In every way to try harder

In climbing
The investment would be a waste
If I did not do that

And am I adept at adjectives?
Writing on a stomach full of hope?
Nine pitches led on a Thursday
After going out on a Tuesday

The best things happen to a climber
Right around ten in the morning
Or right around right now
At nine in the evening
In Squamish
Watching the sun set into the sea

Hip-Hop and Climbing

The fringe is where the magic happens.

Four climbers pack into The Freedom Mobile, a graffitied vehicle, spray-painted red, white, and blue. The sun is shining so brilliantly that it's impossible not to be intoxicated by the vitamin D it provides, even before climbing.

The commute to the crag is filled with excitement and hip-hop, the music of our generation. We are in Indian Creek, Utah, the red rock desert, our home away from home, or home to those that choose to not call civilization home. Red rock walls all around are where we spend our days. The energy of hip-hop is where it's at. The lyrics are secondary, sometimes; it all depends on the mood; sometimes the lyrics are the most important thing. When we're driving to the crag, it's all about the mood, the energy; hip-hop awakes us from the slumber, pumps us up, till people are so damn amped, it must be time to climb.

This scenario unfolded for years, over and over again, before I thought of the connection. Hip-hop has been part of nearly every climbing experience I've ever had. We listen to it on the drive to climbing; the words get stuck in our heads, and nowadays, with iPhones and iPods, music anywhere, anytime, that fits in our pockets, we even listen to hip-hop while climbing. I've been driving around a graffitied car to climbing areas for years, and graffiti is the art that was born with hip-hop in New York City in the 1970s. And, the best of the big climbing parties in our crew of friends always ends up in dance offs. Hip-hop is the soundtrack for my climbing experience, but does the connection just end there? Do hip-hop and climbing have a deeper connection than what is at the surface? Of course they do, but you'll have to go to the fringe of your mind to believe.

Let me climb, let me climb…

—Mos Def, "Climb"

Have you ever listened to the song "Climb" by Mos Def? The cry of the chorus is to "let me climb, let me climb." Yet Mos Def is not a climber, sitting at home in the depths of winter yearning to climb rocks; his yearning comes from a different place, from his soul. What is he trying to climb to, for? Here are some more lyrics from the song:

People climbed up in the night like green trees

They were hanging from the night like green

leaves

Buzzing like queen bees

People climbed into the night like space suits

People stomped inside the night

Stomping and stomping and stomping and

stomping and stomping

Where are they going?

What's the rush?

Everybody in the place was so out of touch

These lyrics are beautiful, infinite, hinting at meaning, yet leaving the listener space to interpret her or his own thoughts on the song. Art. In the sixth months between when I first had this idea to write "Hip-Hop and Climbing" and now, I've listened to this song over and over again to contemplate the lyrics. Something is different each time, depending on my mood, or how much I try to analyze. My conclusion is that climbing is a metaphor; there is no actual climbing taking place, but Mos Def is looking at the nightlife as people climbing out of the daily grind into a different metaphysical landscape, one where they change their clothes, into their "space suits," into the night. The characters of the city are tired of the day-to-day consciousness; they want to be somewhere else; they climb into the night, buzzing like bees. Where does this buzz lead them?

Nighttime is when the things get heavy

You feel alone and you want somebody

Loneliness whispers desperate measures

And you're frantic all by yourself

Nighttime is when the things get heavy

You feel alone and you want somebody

Loneliness whispers desperate measures

Baby don't make no fast moves

Baby don't make no fast moves, tonight

For Mos Def, climbing into the night leads him into the arms of a woman, perhaps one he does not know well. There, with the woman, is that possibility for change in consciousness, yet he is aware of the loneliness, the desperate measures that led the two together. And, then he pauses, wanting to bask in the safety and simplicity of the moment, having a woman in his arms as they sit in the green tree of love that they have climbed into. Then the song fades, and again Mos Def makes the cry to "let me climb, let me climb."

Does it even really matter?

'Cause if life is an uphill battle

We all try to climb on the same old ladder

—B.o.B., "Both of Us"

Where does our desire to climb rocks and mountains come from, and why do we do it? That's one question each and every climber might have a different answer for. Simplified, climbing makes us feel good. No one could argue with that. It is an uplifting activity. Like the change in those who "climbed into the night" in Mos Def's song, there is a change that takes place in the body and mind when we climb. We take our existence in the horizontal, and go vertical.

Like ice, rock, snow, and plastic there are several canvases on which the hip-hopper performs their art. When it began, there was graffiti art, the music, and the dancing. B-boys and b-girls, more commonly referred to as break-dancers in the mainstream, also get vertical, by performing an endless repertoire of moves, and they started this still-popular art form on the horizontal stone of the city, the concrete.

Standing on shaky ground

Too close to the edge

Let's see if I know the ledge

—Rakim, "Know the Ledge"

Hip-hop music is easy to be engaged with; just pump up the volume and there you are; break dancing, on the other hand, is difficult. First off, when you live in a mountain town in Colorado, it's hard to meet break-dancers, and second, break dancing itself is really hard, like 5.13 hard, and if you're really good, 5.14 or 5.15.

My climbing crew has always been infatuated with break dancing, and five years ago, during a rainy Thanksgiving at Indian Creek, we decided to have a dance off. There were only two entrants to the competition, myself and my good friend and climbing partner, Mark Grundon. Both of us had learned our moves from watching break dancing movies, and had a total of two or three moves each in our repertoires. The competition ended when I tried to jump over Mark in the middle of one of his moves, and he stood up. I kicked his neck with a brutal blow, and the competition was over with a major buzz kill. Despite its humble beginnings, every year at Thanksgiving we have a dance off. The rules are stricter, and each climber/dancer gets up to a minute per round to display his or her moves. Some of the climbers in our posse may be 5.12 or even 5.13 climbers, but when it comes to dancing, the best of us is like a 5.9 dancer, maybe 5.9+.

This last year, I wanted to hone my moves some more for the dance off, and I'd moved from the small mountain town of Gunnison, Colorado, to Durango, a much bigger mountain town. We have a couple dance studios, so I called them up searching for break dancing classes. The last one I called did in fact have a class, and at that studio I met my first real break-dancer, Skyhawk.

Where the art form was once invented

On that hardcore pavement in New York

—Large Pro, "Hardcore Hip Hop"

With Tim, a fellow aspiring b-boy, I took some lessons from Skyhawk and fumbled around on the floor to learn some basic moves. When Skyhawk would show us his moves, we saw the dancer we wanted to become. After three months of classes, I had maybe four solid moves in my repertoire. Then after that, something very cosmic happened—I moved into a house with Tim and one of our new roommates was a break-dancer. His name was Cheo, and he was shy in conversation but an animal on the dance floor. He could do windmills, front flips, freezes, and another hundred moves I didn't know the name of. His girlfriend, Jessie, danced as well, and both were into climbing. The universe answered my longtime prayer: to learn how to break dance.

Cheo has a maniacal drive for dancing. His face lights up when he talks about it, and when he dances, he gives every move 110 percent. It is his passion, his favorite thing to do, and what gives him energy to live life. Through Cheo, I met Will, another b-boy, with skills to pay the bills and a very calm and collected demeanor. I got to ask them both many questions about break dancing, and their passion and culture reminded me of hardcore dirtbag climbers.

First off, break dancing takes countless hours of practice, with no financial reward; it's a pursuit of passion, and dancers have to support one another in order for everyone to become better. "You don't do it; you live it," Skyhawk said. "I can spot a break-dancer when I see one on the street with their body language and movement."

"Break dancing helps me stay in shape and stay out of trouble," Cheo shared. "It takes a lot of discipline as well. Dancing makes me happy, and it puts a new energy in my body, gives me energy to stay alive."

Will reminded me of a solo climber. He often practices on his own and for his first three years in Durango didn't even realize there were other break-dancers in town. He started dancing in his grandmother's basement in Brooklyn, New York. "I'm committed to break dancing, and I can't live without it. I like having the community for motivation, but it's a personal thing. I'm fine anywhere."

With access to all these break-dancers, you would imagine my dancing got better, and I was able to impress my climber friends with a wide variety of moves. While I do have a few moves, I learned how much time and dedication it takes to break dance. When it came down to it, I would choose climbing over dancing. That said, like climbing, dancing can still be enjoyed, even if you're only at a 5.7 level. The enjoyment is in the energy, and both climbing and dancing have a unique energy, one that is transforming and empowering.

I'm Zen'd in and I'm zoned out

Tapped in to my own route

—dead prez, "Time Travel"

Energy. Passion. Dedication. These are some words that come to mind when I think about climbing and climbing culture. The break-dancers I know embody these characteristics as well. In the last thirty years, both climbing and hip-hop have grown and are only more and more popular across the globe. Where hip-hop and climbing intersect has to be born in the imagination. Imagining, dreaming, these are essential characteristics to the artist and also to the athlete that embarks in a creative sport that cannot easily be defined.

In modern-day society, there are those that remain happy with the daily grind, and then there are those that have too much angst, too much energy to remain static. These people seek something else. We look beyond, some to the climbing gym, to the cliffs that lie outside of town; others look closer to home, or even within their homes, to the homemade dance floor or to the cipher putting on a show downtown.

The fringe is where the magic happens.

Hip-hop and climbing will continue to define themselves and interact randomly. Like rock 'n' roll did for the generation before mine, hip-hop has given our generation a voice of our own, our own swagger and style that declares: we are different, and we have something to say.

And, in places too numerous to mention, more countries than we could even imagine, a climber might walk past a hip-hopper, and they might look at each other, probably unaware of the energies they share, a random intersection of music, passion, art, and sport.

This piece was originally published in The Climbing Zine, *Volume 5.*

Hit Me Up on My Pager, Yo!

"What is this photo of you doing Jell-O shots?" my mother asked me at a family gathering last year.

She was scrolling through my Facebook photos on her trusty iPad and happened to come by some shots of my recent birthday party. In my midthirties, I'm well past the stage of trying to hide anything from my mom, but I felt the need to offer some context.

"Well, my friend Gala, who has the same birthday as me, found out that I'd never done a Jell-O shot, and she basically forced me to do one," I explained to my dearest mother.

What I didn't explain is that I was scared of Gala. Yes, I'm a grown man, and I'm scared of a woman. Once on Halloween, I was dressed in a woman's sexy-kitten outfit, and Gala was dressed as a zebra. Gala often gets quite aggressive when she's drunk, and I was easy prey. While doing some moves on the dance floor, Zebra Gala ended up kicking me in the face, leading me to the bathroom for ten minutes while I tried to stop a profusely bleeding lip. So when she found out I'd never done a Jell-O shot before and insisted I do one, I didn't try to argue with her.

Sometimes I miss the days when every single little moment was recorded on social media. I come from the last generation that went to college before the social media revolution took off. Which is good, because college is for making mistakes and realizing what type of mistakes you don't want to keep making for the rest of your life. Having my college career on the interwebs for a future employer to see would have probably ensured I would have never gotten a job after graduating.

I also come from the first "screen generation." One of the most thrilling moments of my childhood was when my parents gave in and bought my brother and me a Nintendo. We were obsessed with it, playing Super Mario Bros. and The Legend of Zelda until our parents cut us off. Luckily, we were also into sports, and we had some exercise regimen to combat the stagnant lifestyle that often comes along with video games. Computers came along later, but up until smartphones and social media were invented, they didn't dominate our lives like they do now.

Yes, I come from the last generation of phone callers and note passers. The generation that remembers calling a girl's house and the accompanying fear that her parents might answer. And making mixtapes for a girl, pouring thought into each and every song. When the only way to access adult entertainment was stealing a *Playboy* from someone's dad, and hope to God you didn't get caught. When people had pagers and often used pay phones, and if you were lucky enough, you would get a page that read: *69, which means you were going to get some action.

But I had no game then. I didn't really know how to talk to girls until I was in my early twenties; I was as scared of them as I'm as scared of Gala in a zebra outfit now.

I did have a pager though. A couple of my friends, who were selling dirty-brown brick weed, had pagers, and I wanted to be cool and have money like them and sell weed. Problem was my mom. She found the pager and freaked out. "Drug dealers use pagers," she said.

I thought about trying to angle, saying I was just hoping for a "star 69," but that wouldn't work, and I lost the privilege of a pager.

Part of growing up in my generation means that I was alive when 2Pac and Biggie were alive; these two rappers were both murdered in their twenties and to this day still remain cultural icons. (Their murders are still unsolved as well. WTF?) Just the other day, a twenty-year-old I work with at my night gig at a local restaurant told me, "Dude, that's so cool. You were, like, around when Biggie was alive. What was that like?"

That could have made me feel old, but I guess I'm too young to feel old just yet. I think it's cool that hip-hop is now the oldies, and the original living hip-hop pioneers are now graying and becoming grandfathers.

I do feel blessed that the obsessive recording of every single minute event wasn't going on when I was young. I don't need to see what you had for lunch on my Instagram. Speaking of Instagram, this same twenty-year-old, bless his heart, recently got busted at work for taking shirtless selfies in the bathroom during his shift. When another co-worker, a sixteen-year-old, whose maturity pretty much is the same as the twenty-year-old's, noticed the photos on his Instagram feed when he was eating his shift meal, he made fun of him (as he should). He also called him out for taking the photo at work. The twenty-year-old tried to deny it, but the sixteen-year-old called him out. "You're wearing those same pants, and the background is our bathroom," he said. Busted.

I've never understood the compulsive urge to take a selfie—that's where my generation and the current generation differ—but I can relate to being young and still figuring things out. Lately, I've been hearing this idea that the decision-making part of your brain does not fully develop for a man until around twenty-three years old (slightly earlier for women). This makes such perfect sense as I get older and look back on how I lived my life during my first years of so-called adulthood. What a shame this is! We are forced to make many important life decisions before our frontal lobe fully develops.

These days, there are so many more ways to get in trouble than when I was nurturing my young brain in all the wrong ways. Still, I managed to mostly come out unscathed, my mind fully intact, and most of the photos of my college mistakes are tucked away in a cardboard box up in my attic.

I can't say I'm all that different than some of these kids who didn't know a pre-Facebook world. I like being liked, right swiped, favorited, retweeted, endorsed, and tagged. But I also remember the romance of having to put yourself out there a little bit more, but I doubt any of the girls I made mixtapes for are still holding on to them. It's an ephemeral existence we are living.

I think the main problem with all this new media and technology is thinking that the Instagram photo is more important than the actual moment at hand. My best moments are when I'm away from a cell signal, and thank God, those places still exist. Someday they might not. Or maybe some giant crash will happen, and we'll have to go back to the old ways of living. I think the years before cell phones were more romantic anyways. Either way, I'm damn sure I'll never do another Jell-O shot...unless Gala forces me to!

This piece was originally published in the Durango Telegraph.

If These Walls Could Talk

You could say the Joshua Trees
Planted all the seeds for the dreams
Unwilling to be the same
Unwilling to play the game

And isn't that the way community should be?
Isn't this the place they call the land of the free?

Just fucking close your eyes
And watch the sunrise
Just forget that this
World is full of shit

If these domes could speak
We would get a sneak peek
Of what it would have been like
To solo the walls with such balls
That a rope could be—
A forget me knot

And not just high balls
Climbing it all—
Like Michael Reardon
A light shining as bright
As his hair—
Blond and right on
Like a comet shooting through space

If these boulders could whisper
What would they deliver?
A four-page letter about the better
Things in life: shared food, drink, and laughter
After all, what the fuck else do you need?

Fucking?
Oh yeah, that too
But if these walls could talk
They'd prefer making love

Because there's enough fucking fucking
Going on in this goddamned world

Yeah the love that has been made
That's the shit
That's the IT
That's what make the J Trees
Get their swerve on
Leaning toward the infinite

If the Cyclops could talk
It might reminisce over you
And the thousands of others
That looked through its eye
And saw the light, the hope

If Course and Buggy could speak
It would teach
The way Peter Croft
Practiced his craft
And found the oneness
The Buddha would have been proud of

If these boulders could whisper
They would surely deliver
Stories of lovers like puzzles
Two pieces locked together
And rocked the boat
All night long
And then looked to the stars
For dessert

If Hidden Valley could rally
Back twenty years ago
To a young Dean Potter
And meet the necessity of his invention
Of his perplexing desire to fly
But of course the first man to fly, had to die
But that can't stop the tears from my eye

Just like the first people to climb
On ropes made of twine and hemp
Ate up so much danger they either became
Full of fear or fearless
But less is more and it's more likely
Their consciousness carried a touch of gray

So let's take it there

While urban contemporaries
Write that the dirtbag is dead
On their Apple computers
Made of precious metals
Here in J Tree, there are ten and twenty
Women and men
Living out of bags
In the dirt
It's that simple
The dirtbag is alive

If these walls could talk
They would tell us
No one ever complained
Back in the day
No one ever had the luxury
To hate the unforgiveness
Of slabby granite mixed with sweat
After all, it was all that existed
Before climbing went sport
Before climbing went plastic

J Tree just brings the truth to life
And some people don't like
What they see when they look into
The reflection of direction
That a Joshua Tree points to
Some people don't like it
That a Joshua Tree lives longer
Than they will
So that's why we kill

But if we accept what the trees speak
We can write poetry 'til infinity

So who are we?
Are we hippie?
Are we hobo?
Beatnik or dirtbag?
We are in Cali
So we can be
All these
We can be
Whatever
We want to be
If this is the land of the free

If these domes
Let their minds roam
They would tell us to come home
Come home

Come back to that place
In your heart that is
The hardest to get to
Sometimes

Come back to the desert
Come back to the skeleton
Get away from four walls
And listen to the walls

Free Moab (and Boulder)

Utah and Colorado. We are neighbors, and many of us go back and forth between our borders so often it's hard to know which place to call home. Sure, the government makes us all have an address to claim, but that feeling that overtakes you when you arrive at your favorite red rock destination feels a lot like home too, doesn't it?

I call both places home in my heart: the campsites, washes, and walls of Indian Creek provide a true sense of place and meaning during the spring and fall, and the house I rent in Durango provides a more permanent sense of establishment when the desert is either too hot or too cold. I still hold down a couple steady-paying gigs in Durango during desert season (writing and rolling burritos), so that two-and-a-half-hour drive is like a weekly commute. It's a lot of driving, but there are worse commutes in the world, don't you think?

Growing up in the Midwest, I'd heard of Colorado, of course, but I don't know how much I really knew about Utah, other than it was that place Jerry Garcia sang about in "Friend of The Devil" where he "spent a night in Utah in a cave up in the hills."

Come to think of it, some twenty years after I first heard that lyric, and of Utah, it still rings true—it's a place, once you know that red rock matrix well, you could do such a thing, and no one would ever know you were there.

Once you come down to town, back to that so-called reality, Utah shows a different kind of flavor, one rooted in weirdness, a religiously conservative nature, and harsh laws if you are a hedonist, like many of us Colorado folks are (read: you like to smoke weed and drink beer). You want to buy a beer? Too bad it's warm. You want to smoke some weed? Well, there's a $1,000 fine for that here.

That's something we Colorado folk learn as "part of the deal" in Utah. Be careful. They are looking for you and want your money. And really that's all you have to do: be careful, don't give them probable cause, and you're good to go.

In the last few years since Colorado legalized the devil's weed and created an empire around the plant, boosting our economy, and keeping people out of the criminal system that should have never been there (you should try it, Utah), the philosophical gap between the two states seems to have widened. This became evident in the most concrete of ways a dirtbag philosopher such as myself happened to notice: a bumper sticker. It read: FREE MOAB, set inside a mock-up of the Colorado flag.

And, while we're talking about us sinners, can I take a tangent to mention a section of highway that takes one from Durango to Indian Creek used to be called 666 before they renamed it, for a variety of reasons, one of those being that 666 is the "number of the beast." Oddly enough, 6 is my lucky number, so I've never been afraid of the dreaded 666—in fact, I kinda like it.

Anywho, what were we talking about? Weed. Yeah. No, wait Moab, and the people who want to free it, which I imagine some longtime Moab folks felt quite amused by. Who do these Colorado folks think they are? They don't even live here, and they want to shape the culture. They define our seasons, as in the old joke: How do you know when the seasons are changing? When the license plates start turning green.

Much like Austin seems to be for Texas, Moab is for Utah—a relatively hip place in an overly conservative state. And that's what the true differences are in Colorado versus Utah, right? A difference in political beliefs. Utah's history is unique to any other place because it was shaped by the Mormon religion (you know, the LSDs), a group of people who fled persecution all the way from the East Coast to the Wild West, where the founders discovered a place that would let them have forty wives (well, for a little while). You can still see the sad remnants of that lifestyle in places like Colorado City.

So, now we have a movement, albeit a bumper sticker movement—in the interest of full disclosure, my friend made said stickers—to Free Moab from the unjust laws and odd culture of Utah. (Warm beer is un-American, dammit).

At the same time while all of this is going on, you have the Republican Congressman Rob Bishop advocating a bill to turn over federal land to the state of Utah, so that the state can develop this land in a variety of ways. And, all of this got me thinking; maybe Utah and Colorado could work something out with this Free Moab movement. Maybe we could give Utah something in return.

How about Boulder?

Now don't get it twisted—I like Boulder. It's a cool mountain town that was probably cooler before it became defined as a cool town, but it's still a great place. But, Boulder suffers from a phenomenon I'll greatly reduce for the sake of brevity: "too many pretentious hippies." You see, hippies, like the Mormons, are great. They are nice, and although they don't always smell the best, they usually have good intentions. They have their own unique set of beliefs and want to save the world in their own little way. Hey, at least someone's trying to save this damned planet! (Let me also add that if I have to decide on a religious belief, I'm going to pick Hippie. If I'm going to be in eternal heaven, I think I want the noodling of Jerry Garcia there.)

So, Utah is too stiff, too rigid, and too conservative. And, Colorado, especially Boulder, well, sometimes we are too loose, too stoned, and on the verge of too liberal. Why don't we mix it up? Nothing good has ever happened from large groups of hippies. Well, maybe except the Grateful Dead and Dr. Bronner's soap. Which begs the question, if so many hippies use Dr. Bronner's, why do they always smell so bad? If a hippie takes a shower in the woods and he still smells, did that shower actually happen?

What I'm getting at is that these two cultures (the Mormons and the hippies/dirtbags) are bound to clash, and maybe if we got together and comingled these cultures, there would be a better balance.

If I can digress, the native people of these lands used the land in a much more natural, effective way, in a similar yet less-destructive and environmentally consumptive way, migrating to the mountains when it got hot in the desert and back to the lower elevations in the winter. They had shit figured out, that's for sure, 'til the white man and his crazy ideas came along.

Now, as I'm finishing up this article, and doing some research, aka Googling, and wait, Brendan Leonard, that Semi-Rad guy, has already thought this subject through more than I have. (Insert, my fist shaking at the proverbial sky with Brendan's face in the clouds.) His idea: a megastate, Utahlorado. Just merge it all. No more Free Moab. No more stereotypical Coloradoans. Just one place of awesomeness.

"And think about the license plate options," Leonard writes. "Peyton Manning throwing a football through Delicate Arch? Or maybe the green mountains of Colorado's current license plates with "UtahloRADo" on them, celebrating the addition of the word 'rad' to Utahans' new home state? Musicians covering 'Rocky Mountain High' would only have to add one syllable to the chorus, which wouldn't be so awkward. Try it once: 'Rocky Mountain High, Utah-loradooooo.'"

This piece was originally published in the Utah Adventure Journal.

The Gobie

I'm working on my faults and cracks

Filling in the blanks and gaps

And when I write them out they don't make sense

I need you to pencil in the rest

—Frightened Rabbit, "My Backwards Walk"

I looked at my hand, the gobie that was once an open cut now nearly a completely healed wound. Of course, it was from Indian Creek, world-famous home of the gobie. Out there, it was a game changer—no more .75 finger stacks on the project. But, almost a week removed, I had a sort of sentimentality for it—the gobie was a physical reminder of two extremely peaceful days in the midst of a two-week climbing trip.

Georgie says all my writing is about climbing and women, and everything circles back to that. I never really realized that until she said it, and then it was as clear as day—she was right as fuck. These last seventeen years that I've been a climber have not just been about those two things though—they have been a spiritual journey. Don't worry. I'm not going to get all Deepak Chopra on your ass; it's just the truth—the outdoors unlocked the keys to seeing my true self. And, I'm still looking into that mirror.

The journey toward meeting your true self is often described as an inner journey, and there's a lot of truth to it. But, in the world of climbing, you really can't do anything on your own. Every success is built within the community. Someone, Georgie, had to nudge me back on that trail toward the real me.

That gobie: I know exactly where it came from, right at the top of my latest Indian Creek project. I was only on toprope, but I was making some horrific, grunting, chuffer noises. Screaming— *eaaaahhhhhh, uuuunnnhhhh, ahahhhhhhahhh*—you know, those weird noises that come from Indian Creek that are kinda like sex noises, primal and reflecting a profound effort of the essence of climbing— that trying-hard thing. Trying hard is the best.

So I tried hard and screamed, and Georgie was the only one to hear. We were in a remote part of Indian Creek, not rare, not that hard to get to, just an isolated spot where everything you do is work, so not many people go back there. Climbing becomes blue collar when you're putting up new routes in remote corners, but you're rewarded with a long-forgotten silence and solitude that most don't get in the modern Creek experience.

That gobie—it's so close to healed now and it will be fully healed when I go back out to the Creek next weekend. It was annoying when it happened, but as the wound closes up, there's a memory in there I don't want to let go of—the memory of those two days with her, alone in the desert.

I'd already killed the vibe of romance. I said some foolish things. Most notably, I asked her if she was ready to start a relationship with me, like four days into the trip. When she said she didn't know, I got mad and defensive. We were in Joshua Tree then, another place like Indian Creek where, when you tap into the silence, you can't hide from your true self once you're tapped in. And, the reality was, my true self was deeply suffering from fear and attachment. It had been there for some time now, but that fateful day, Georgie exposed it like a splitter crack.

Part of the reason I write about women so much is that for, like, the first seven years of my dating life I felt mostly pain, with very short glimpses and moments of happiness. The other part is that I simply love women, and I'm a hopeless romantic. Basically I was just figuring out women (I still am).

After all, women are the greatest mystery.

My friend Joy told me those words just before I left on the trip. She was the one who encouraged me to write Georgie back after she'd mailed me a short thank-you note for some editing I'd done for her, while also hinting she had a crush on me. Joy is happily married, and I could tell she enjoyed the prospect of helping me start off a new romance.

And how have I gotten this far and not written about what I adore about Georgie. That's so like me to talk about myself. The thing for me that draws me in with Georgie is her energy and her openness. She's the type of person you feel like you can tell anything to. She looks you in the eyes and hopes for the same from you. She is full of love and shares it freely.

She's so encouraging when she's belaying you that it feels like she wants you to succeed just as much as you want to succeed. She's fucking funny, and in those two weeks we spent getting to know each other on the rocks and the road, I can't recall laughing that much in a long time.

She has this presence that makes you present and a mind that can stimulate every intellectual pleasure center I can think of. She will talk of her grandmother and her love of dogs in the same two sentences. Any girl that talks about her grandma and dogs on a first date is a good woman. And, you should see her when she sees a sweet dog—that look in her eyes will make you believe in a higher power, or at least believe in love.

She's the voice of the modern climbing feminist and can rile up a group of readers like no other. She is at her best in conversation when she is unfiltered. She is the best in writing when she thinks it through. People on the Internet might not like her, but I don't know how they could not like her if they met her.

She tells me she has flaws and has had immense struggles, but she makes everything look so easy that you would never believe it. Georgie will speak up when something is not right in a climbing situation, and she has everyone's back. She loves climbing so fucking much, and if you do to, for all the reasons, she'll maul you like a bear with enthusiasm. She gets tired too, though. She will go on and on about everything all day, but then she will need her space. Pearl, her Subaru, will do that for her; it seems to be enough. She's lived out of it for years now. She's a real fucking dirtbag, that Georgie. Doesn't even use a damn cooler.

Her friends say she puts the *dirt* in *dirtbag*. But damn, that girl always smells so good. I mean, what the fuck, is it pheromones or what? That's smell. Oh, that smell, that smell of a woman you love. Ah, fuck, now I'm crying and getting all fucking sentimental. But, Georgie wants me to write through the tears, I know, so I will.

Georgie is one of my favorite writers—not writers that I know, or those that I work with, but simply one of my favorites. She has a voice in world and scene that is desperately lacking voice. It's deeper than that for me with her, because she is my favorite person to write TO. And, who do we even write to anymore? Grandma a few times a year? And, I'm not talking e-mails; I'm talking writing, sitting down with your brain and your self and your feelings and just putting it all on paper.

And, now I'm getting to the heart of it, because my crush with Georgie began by letter writing. We would go back and forth, even before we met, and tell each other about ourselves and our feelings for each other (wherever the fuck those were coming from). It was like she was healing the pain from my past every time she signed, sealed, and delivered a little note to my post-office box.

For some reason, after all these years, I was still holding on to that pain from years past, like a child holding on to a stuffed animal or a blanket too long. It had to be let go. I've loved many incredible women since my younger heartbroken days, and those women are enough for me to believe in love again, rather than going to the dark place that is self-pity.

But, she called me out, and it was tough to hear. She told me there was no way I could know her well enough to want to start a relationship. She told me that, in reality, it had nothing to do with her; it was me; I wanted to protect myself from future pain by controlling the situation in a direction that had only one outcome: us starting a relationship together.

90

I'll never forget that day, because in all of my adult life, I can't recall words I've wanted to take back so badly. I mean, dude, what the fuck were you thinking? Telling this beautiful woman that you are enamored with that she has let you down because she won't commit to a relationship a week into knowing you? But I know, now, it was never about her—it was about that pain I thought was gone, but it was still in my heart.

We were walking in solitude, in Joshua Tree, that skeleton of a desert that gives by taking away. We were looking for a classic splitter crack, seeking the simplicity of beauty by attempting to climb something so difficult, yet easy. All you gotta do is crank down on those jams and figure out a way to make it a dance. And that's all that the beginning days of love are, a little dance to see if you are in rhythm, and I had it, and then I stepped all over her toes, and her heart.

From trying to control the situation, I immediately lost my chance to love her in a romantic way, at least on that trip. And, that gobie is the last little reminder of the time before I'd messed it up.

I've always struggled with attachment, but I've known the feeling for so long that I failed to realize it was a problem to see my true self. And it took a true friend to help me see that. It took Georgie to help me get back on my spiritual path.

A big part of me wishes I could go back to that hike to give that Former Me a pep talk. "Dude, you had a broken heart, but it's healing now. Can't you see that? Can't you see what you went through was so minor compared to what some people go through? Don't hold on to that shit, and more importantly, don't make your shit someone else's shit. Can't you see how innocent and awesome those first days of infatuation are? Just savor it, man, the journey of a thousand miles begins with one step…"

Like my heart, the gobie needs to heal; I think I'll put some salve on it now. Time marches forward, and we are all destined to be dust here in a few years. Everything good must end. Hanging on only provides pain.

I can't go back and give that guy I call Former Me a pep talk. That's just not the way the world works. Time marches on, whether it be slow like a Bob Dylan love song or fast like the new Kanye beat. But I can talk to the Current Me, the only me that will ever exist until I pass on and only my words and stories remain. I can tell him it's okay he fucked up. She forgives you. You still get to talk and write with her almost every day. It was a pipedream of a romance, and the feeling was so deep that someone was going to get their feelings hurt. She lives in California, dude. You love Colorado, and you have spent a long time building your life there. You were looking for love, and you found it. You love her, and she loves you; it's just that we can't package love up the way we idealize it. Love is love, and it ceases to be love when it's controlled. Like rappelling off a rope and surviving, you finally learned that lesson. And, look at you, breathing, surviving, going climbing soon, the entire world of life and love is still in your grasp.

But wait—let's bring it back to climbing, where hanging on is rewarded. The best climbers are simply the ones that can hang on the longest. Climbing is this yin and yang thing though. Knowing when to fight and when to back off can be the difference between life and death, success and failure. And, never forget that the best climbing moments kinda feel like floating anyways, a profound act of trying without trying. Just doing. Just like making love. Becoming one with something else.

The project still awaits. It still sits there in the middle of nowhere, which for the soul climber, is the middle of everywhere. The gobie needs to heal so I can have another battle. The gobie will heal. And, you know what, my heart will heal; it was hurting so long I got used to the feeling and called it a friend instead of an enemy.

And, I'll climb. Unattached. Sure, there will be the rope and the gear, but in the best moments when we are climbing, we don't even need these things. Just like our best moments of love, we are so truly in the moment that the past and the future don't even exist. That's living. That's loving. That's climbing.

Just For You

This isn't poetry
This is acid rap
Mixed with Kerouac

Take a Chance
Drafting of the poets
I'm the number-seven pick

I'll keep going
On and on like Badu
I'll keep going
Just for you

Usually I quit after
Just a minute
Of writing poetry
'Cause I can't write just for me
It's gotta be just for you

And sometimes it's like you're the last other poet left
'Cause somewhere poetry got left behind

But my mind
With
Your mind
We bringing it back

But I ain't no minute man
I am just a man who has a minute
Yet I'll hint at the infinite
Just for you

Just because I'm on a plane
And my brain was drifting back
To that time you gave me brain
And I was tilted back
Unto the heavens
And then I was gonna give it back

Just to you

Tasting you
Tasting me
Just you and me

Because now we be
Existing in different spaces
Different places
Like we always been
And is it true?
I've only known you
For two months
Or was it two beers
Every night for two weeks
Too sweet, too good
Highs gotta have the lows

We packed in two years
And soon I knew
Someday I'd write
Just for you

But you only wanted poetry
And I only had poetry
To give
Perfect.

She had the booze
I had the chronic
Everything was yonic.

You know when it's me
And I know when it's you
Something true
Writing
Just for you

Does this leap off the page?
And give you a hug?

Show you some love?

Could it be?
Like morning coffee
Mixed with a sunrise
That made your eyes
All fucking teary

Clearly this was not
Meant for no page
This is burning sage
And plays
On summer nights that extended
As far as the heavens would let it
'Cause it resembled eternity
Can't you see
This is
Just for you

This is the middle of a runout
When the only choice that can be
Is to be

Can't you see?
This is a Nelly beat
Two beers deep
On a summer night
You know that summer right

Can I get a semicolon?

This is two thousand feet up above
The valley floor
With much more to go;
Many moons to love

This is uncomfortable
Un-Instagrammable
#unhashtaggable
unformattable

But not unfuckable
But unfuckwithable

This is unfucking
Un-anything
That doesn't make you think
You aren't as sharp
As a kitchen knife
Cutting through disillusion
As calm as the stillest ocean
As beautiful as perfect splitters
Like that perfect hotness
In the feminine or male
'Cause you gotta have something in that splitter
To fill it
That was a lot of double negatives
When in reality all I got is positive
For you

And I'm positive
I'm not even writing this
So who is?
Or what is?
Or we is?

Look at this
Who the fuck
Do I think I is?
Some fucking poet?
No, fuck that
I'm not even writing this

Take the me
Out of poetry
And you get the we

We
Flying
Riding
Out

To
Sunset

And where do you wanna be?
Where you wanna go?
'Cause I got dat Subaru you know.
And it knows where the splitters go

'Cause this shit is splitter
Put your hands in it
Feel it, jam it
Man it
Feels good to be a gangster
Of Love
Yeah I capitalized that shit
Cause I'm a motherfucking pimp
Pimping these bitches I call words
Just for you

It's true
What do you want to make them do?
Get you off?
Get it on?
Turn them off and on
Like a light switch

How about we twerk 'em
And tweak 'em
Make 'em show what they
Working with

These aren't words or verbs
Or cusses or cussing
Or fighting or fucking
It's much deeper than that
Much higher
Much lighter
Like air

Fuck, breathe for a second

Fuck that, breathe for a minute
Breathe like it's your fucking job
Cause it is

You fucking know what I mean
When I say fuck, so fuck it
Can I get an em dash?

Are you still there?

Listening—Reading—Feeling?

Do you want to see where this
Reading is leading you?

I did write this
Just for you
'Cause it's just me
On this plane
On this brain
Listening to its heart

You know this whole poem is heart
Is blood pumping
Blood spilling
Blood drying
Blood never lies

But I do
But I never lie in poetry
I just lie to me
In that space between the heart

——

And the brain

——

But it's time

It's high time
We take the me
Out of poetry
After all, this is
Just for you

The Gobie Heals

It felt a little bit weird that a relative stranger had changed my life. A new era of self-exploration had begun. After exposing Georgie to all my bullshit that I should have dealt with on my own, I learned of her own trials and tribulations, but of course, those are her stories to tell, not mine. I only have my story. Someday, though, mark my words, we will see a great book from her brilliant, loving mind.

I started paying attention to my heart more. I wanted to act out of pure love rather than fear. I wanted to live in the moment, not out of regret from the past. This, of course, is a lifelong journey, and every day is a challenge. I did go back to the past and analyzed when I was acting irrationally in relationships. At the same time, I was glad to still be single—sometimes you can really only truly grow when you're on your own. But through all the contemplation, I realized, as I have many times before, that a loving relationship would be key to my happiness; the deeper realization, though, is that I've needed to arrive at my true self before I could ever be a good partner to someone else.

With spring coming to a close, I ventured out to the desert for my last trip of the season. Coincidentally, or not, Georgie was there too. She'd been dreaming of desert splitters all spring in California. She rallied her posse, and I rallied mine, and we came together as one unified crew in Indian Creek.

We'd agreed to be friends. That was hard for me. She'd rejected me, and typically when that happens, I shut my heart off to that person, and I usually cut them out of my life until I'm over them. But, by then it's too late to salvage a friendship. Something was different. I wanted to shut Georgie out, but my heart would not let me.

So, we moved into friendship. We helped each other out with our writing, and she became a go-to editor. Friends heard about our crazy two-week-first-date adventure, and I'd talk about her. Everyone was always asking about her; I wasn't quite sure why. The part of me drawn to fear wanted to completely forget about her. Something, in some way, would not let that happen. There's always been something cryptic about Georgie, like we were destined to meet.

The project, The King, was the only thing on my mind more than her that spring. She'd helped me kick off the season on that, when the massive gobie stopped my progress for a couple weeks. But I kept getting on the line, thinking that maybe, just maybe, in a few years it would go down.

Vision is the thing in climbing. One day, while working on the improbably desperate start to The King, a 5.13 crack that demanded liebacking and pinky-tip jams, I looked over to the right and finally saw that area of the rock in a new way—it looked like there could be a more reasonable start twenty feet over that led into the main headwall.

I gave it a toprope go, and the moves were incredible, finishing with a tricky and heady mantle. That day, we had just an hour or so left in our session, but both of my partners, Tim and Gene, agreed we needed to bolt this alternate start. Since it was way off to the right, it was tough to get a stance to drill. (I was drilling on toprope to get the bolts in just the right place.) Tim came up with the idea for him to give me a belay from the right side, keeping the tension in a perfect way that allowed me to hang exactly where I wanted and drill. The metaphor was not lost. It was a team effort, and we got the alternate start installed.

Looking back on my climbing life, I know I'm a bit of a lazy climber. I like climbing as a pastime just as much as I enjoy anything else. Only in the last couple years have I started to really dig deep and try projects over and over until I send them. Somehow, now, at thirty-seven years old, I'm climbing harder than I ever have. Perhaps it's physiology, or the motivation that the clock is ticking for hard climbing, or maybe it's that carrot that dangles at the top of a first ascent.

Now that The King had this alternative start, it went from being a farfetched dream to something I could climb this season, with a little luck. After the bolted start, the climb has a soaring, steep, and sometimes offset .75 Camalot crack on a headwall for eighty-five some feet. The line itself looks like an artist created it; well, I guess the original artist, Mother Nature, did create it. The King was inspirational, intimidating, and intimate, both a literal lightning bolt, and an exclamation point, in the form of a crack.

That last weekend of the season, my heart was fluttering, and we had a solid crew of friends, new and old. Everyone agreed I should try to send The King, and thus we set up our little basecamp there once we hiked up to the Cave Wall. Georgie gave me a belay on my first burn.

I had butterflies, and on that first go, my jitters got the best of me when I fell out of the first crux, a couple of one-inch finger jams that led to the main headwall. I wasn't putting my feet in the crack. That's what I love about these hard cracks: you've got to focus in on each and every move.

In all of my years of climbing, it's rare to find a partner that truly wants you to succeed as much as you want to succeed. But Georgie is that person. She would say these things: tell me to breathe, to relax at just the right moment, in just the right tone. She is a climbing partner that inspires me to become the best climber I can be.

The rest of the climb went well; I think I fell, like, one more time. It felt good; it felt within my grasp—Georgie's stoke fueled mine; in fact, everyone who was up there that day fueled the stoke.

I love it when life has a few precious hours hanging in the balance and you have just that time to do what you need to do. It was the last weekend in May; Creek season was slipping away. Usually, The King goes into the sun around midafternoon, but this particular day, we were blessed with some cloud cover and a breeze. Conditions would allow one last attempt for the season.

Tim gave me a belay this time. He is also one of those people who want you to succeed as much as you want to succeed. When he belays me, he's on board 100 percent, sending good vibes and encouraging words. I climbed the start, again feeling nervous and uneasy but trying to breathe, trying to float up the rock. I knew I was going to give this thing everything I had.

I made it past the first finger-crack crux and embarked onto the headwall. What followed was the most surreal feelings I've ever experienced in a pitch at The Creek. After the finger-crack crux, I climbed into a section of butterfly jams, and it continually felt like the crack was trying to spit me out. Everything felt desperate, and it started to feel more and more like I was out of my body, while fully feeling and experiencing everything the climb had to offer. Suddenly, as I was pulling a move above a small bulge to a semirest, I felt a cramp in my left arm—*No way would it go down now*, I thought, but I managed to pull the bulge, maxing out in every way. This "rest" consisted of a decent foot out right and jamming my left toe painfully in a pod, while balancing with one butterfly jam in the crack in front of me. I looked up at the next section, more offset butterfly jams, tight .75 cams, and thought there was no way I could do it. But, I kept thinking that, and I kept climbing. More and more, I felt energy coming from another place. From the ground, from friends that helped me work the route— I was pulling positive energy out of everywhere I could.

The climbing felt desperate, yet I knew exactly what I needed to do: to stay in the crack. At this point, all of the crew at the crag was watching me, saying positive things, encouraging the good fight. I'd known this feeling before, trying so hard, all for the sake of trying hard, all for the sake of how good that feels. More and more, it was not me who was up there. I can't explain that now, not ever, but when I finally reached the more forgiving finger jams up higher, I knew there was no way in the world I would fail, that I would let go. I clipped the chains, and yelled to everybody, "That wasn't me. I don't know who that was, but it wasn't me…"

It really felt beyond me, a silly thing to say about a silly little crack, that we silly people who call ourselves climbers pursue. But, damn, did it leave me smiling. Down the winding trail, we inched toward the celebratory beer. I purposely walked first, ahead of everyone, so I could just be in my own head, smiling, proud of myself, and happy—I just wanted to enjoy that headspace for a minute. I'd been fighting for myself and my climbing all spring. It was just time to enjoy that moment in the purest place I know, Indian Creek.

Wrapping up that project, I realized how silly a one-pitch project is in itself; I almost felt a tinge of feeling sorry for the professional climbers who define their lives by these little chunks of rock, even more sorry for the boulderers. But, ha, there is a Zen lesson at the heart of it, because sometimes the divine exists in the silliness. That something so insignificant in the larger realm of things can be so meaningful.

This meaningful journey on yet just another crack in a rock made me realize, once and for all, the yardstick by which we measure something being "hard" as climbers is kinda silly. A couple days later, I tried The Optimator, a 5.13 finger crack. It felt easier than The King. So that meant my route might check in somewhere around that grade. Had I been a young man, it would have gone straight to my ego. But here I was, older, at an age where if I listened to society, my athletic abilities should be going downhill. But, they weren't; I was getting better. And, I knew deep inside that I still had more to give to the craft. And that day, after a good burn on The Optimator, I knew I would. The rest of my days of trying hard things had to be dedicated to the improvement of my craft, not my ego. For the ego is never satisfied and always wants more, but doing it for the craft takes it back to the pastime, and that place knows the importance of soaking into your moment in time; for that time will be over before you know it, the beautiful sunset seeping into darkness. And as a climber, I certainly know the darkness, all climbers who have spent time on tall walls do.

But the "I" part is what I would later question the most. With a hard climbing project, there must be a certain level of psyche and motivation. Some people can cultivate this on their own, but I need to share it. I need that extra energy and support, that love. And I've needed it in life, just as much, or even more, than with a climb.

In the deep of the bullshit that I exposed Georgie to, I expressed to her that if it wasn't going to work out between us, I was done living this life with an open heart; I was done believing in love; surely there had to be another way, right? I could just find a beautiful woman who would never ask to see my heart and only would provide love for me but would never confront the ways I am damaging to myself. I wanted that. For a moment, with an aching heart, full of the truth, I really wanted that. I wanted a house for my heart, with walls all around it for protection, and the shield armor of a woman who would protect my vulnerabilities from the world.

She told me there was no way I would ever be like that. She said my heart would never accept it. She said having an open heart to the world is both the best and the worst thing in the world. God dammit, that girl was right.

But there was a long silence in that phone conversation. My heart was depleted at that particular moment. You know that silence in a phone conversation that can only happen with someone you've shared intimate moments with. That silence of eternity. That silence of brutal honesty.

Understood. All my life, I've just wanted others to understand my heart; I want to understand my heart. When Georgie came out of nowhere, and we started writing each other, I instinctually knew she understood me, before we'd even met. It was the trippiest of feelings but also a confirmation that we share something very special as a human race: we share an understanding of certain people and things; who that aligns with provides the greatest mysteries and excitements of life. That belief that someone who completely understands you could just be right around the corner. The fact that many of us don't really understand one another begs another rabbit hole of questions. But that is life, isn't it?

What I've understood, and learned this year, this rollercoaster of a year, is that the pain and the joy live in the same place, so close they form a circle; perhaps that is what the whole yin and yang thing is about. The place you've felt so much pain is the source of the future joy. And, in climbing, where all the metaphors come and go, all the trying and the effort that we sometimes call failure leads to that word we call success. And, somehow, I get the feeling those words are both misleading and misguiding in their nature. So, in climbing and in love, we must pay attention to the heart and try to learn the language it is speaking.

Tons of Guns

Guns Guns Guns
Tons of Guns
But I got none

Decided to go with the pen
Even though I know
The Gun is mightier than the pen
Didn't get it?
I'll reiterate it again

The Gun is mightier than the pen

But maybe not the sword
But who has swords anymore?
Maybe not since the .com
Or since the atomic bomb

Cuz we are all dumb and we say shit is the bomb
When really dropping bombs in the worst thing we do
And we all light off fireworks and act like it's cool

But, fuck I was
Born into this
Even born into privilege
In Normal, Illinois

Had I been born
In the south side of Chicago

I would have a gun.

But what if I wanted to do something?
To change this course we are on
Or have we already set sail, to jail?

Shit I gotta
Take a deep breath
Cause I don't

Write like this anymore

Not since college

But two days ago
My brother's brother-in-law
A good but bipolar man
Shot himself.

None of that rhymed
But I ain't got the time
Or the timing
To make everything drop on a dime
That's fine

But this situation isn't
And my poetry
Won't change the world

I am just some local poet
With a thousand Facebook fans.
My death might not even make the New York Times.

Lately I've been studying World War II
Fuck it was worse then
I'm surprised the Earth survives
But that's what it does
That's what we do

Another death
In the Midwest
Bipolar

A mother, father, sister, brother
Crying
The only words I ever remember
Ben saying was at a wedding
"I want to welcome you to the family"

So there I am at the funeral

Really a member of this family

His sister is pregnant
A little girl
I'm going to be an uncle
In this troubled world

And all I want to do
Is live more
All the time

When someone dies
And you cry
Uncontrollably
Who do you call?
Seriously,
Who do you call?

I wish we could pack up
All the human killing guns
And sink them in the bottom of the sea
Or better yet recycling

Turn the steel
Into cars
That we could drive far
And make love under stars

I wish we could
Detonate hate
And disarm
All nuclear arms

I wish the pen
Was mightier than the sword
Or I wish there were still swords

I wish my words
Were more than words

Good-bye, Indian Creek
A Series of Vignettes

Ran into the devil, babe,

He loaned me twenty bills

I spent that night in Utah

In a cave up in the hills

—Grateful Dead, "Friend of The Devil"

I shotgunned a beer for the first time the other night.

Not something I ever really expected to do since I'm thirty-seven years old, and I've never been good at beer chugging—but I decided what the hell—this is the last time I'll ever stay in the Creek Pasture campsite in Indian Creek for free again. Plus, it was Utah 3.2 beer, and that stuff is mostly water anyways.

It was one of those nights when you stop and think that the next time you come back to the place it will be changed. What's changing is not the worst thing in the world: the BLM is starting to charge five bucks a night per site to stay here in the fall. It is, however, worth noting that Indian Creek was the last major climbing destination in the United States that did not charge for camping. But, our tribe is growing, services must be maintained, and those services are not free, which of course begs the age-old question, Is freedom really free? Well, there's a price for being free, that's for sure. But yeah, freedom should be free. So should love. We live in a complex world.

I've been climbing out at Indian Creek for almost two decades now, something that, when I share that with younger climbers, makes me sound old school. I like that in a way, and when I'm around these youngsters coming up in the climbing world, I like to tell them stories. Even when I'm a few beers deep, with a decent buzz, I always have an agenda with my stories. With a lot of these younger climbers, I sense a hunger, and if I don't see that hunger, I honestly don't end up spending that much time with them—the person who doesn't have hunger and desire is never going to achieve anything in the realm of climbing. Mostly what I want young Creek aficionados to understand is the value of struggling to achieve their goals out here, and a respect for the land.

I wish I could connect with more of them, because I know there are so many "new" Indian Creek climbers and, comparably, so few veteran climbers. The mentorship component in climbing has a hard time keeping up with our sport's exploding popularity. The climbing in Indian Creek gets more popular every year, and the user visits increase every year as well.

The crack-climbing masochism of Indian Creek is an acquired taste, to say the least. It's kinda surprising how popular it is, considering how painful it can be. I knew I loved it from day one, back in 1999, but I never actually thought I'd figure it out. I hung after every other jam, back then, on my first trip. I knew the landscape had spirits though, positive ones, and I knew there was something healing about it, as weird as that seems to write about a place that so often inflicts bruises and wounds on its suitors.

The acquired taste, the seasoning of the soul to grow and love the place, can take so long that I really feel like this last season was when I finally, once and for all, truly fell in love with it. And just before it was all about to change.

The Burnout

It was many, many years before I realized that this environment was the ultimate. I just didn't see it. The climbing was too hard, too painful, too demanding. Perhaps I just had to get through the fire, the burnout, before I fell in love.

I remember a beer run to Moab early on. I figured I'd get some more cigarettes; I was getting low. I was running on empty for some time in that late 1990s era, and the pack of ciggies I smoked every day was the constant metaphor and reminder that my life would never be shit. I'd taken off from home in the Midwest in the most dramatic of fashions, suicidal and thinking that life was about to be over. If only I'd known then that that was only the beginning.

Well, the beer run was the longest of my life, a full two hours there and back. I remember the twists and turns at that one hairpin curve, and how after that point, it was a different world—no longer just cows, deer, sagebrush, and juniper trees. There were crimson walls of glory with the most unforgiving crack climbs you've ever seen.

I recall camping at the lower Bridger Jack campsites, sites that are now closed off. I recall the older climbers talking of bigger objectives, and mostly, I recall a statement that one of them made about forgetting what month it was. There was a kind of brilliant, beautiful absentmindedness to this lifestyle. I remember how they would use their old juice bottles as their water bottles. I remember when the trip was coming to an end, all they would talk about was when they would return. They all lived up in Laramie, Wyoming, and it seemed crazy that they would drive two states away just to climb some cracks. But I didn't know then what I know now.

Five years and a bachelor's degree later, I was starting to get it. In fact, it was all I got. So, I was on the road and living in my brand-new tent in that same Bridger Jack campground where I'd seen the preview of my life unfold, even if I didn't realize it at the time, which of course we rarely do.

I was off the cigarettes and off those delusional thoughts of suicide and turmoil. I was tuning in to the belief that life had something to really offer, but I'd still hadn't found the balance yet. I was climbing with random people when my buddies weren't around, but most of the time, I did have friends around. The climbing life isn't much without good friends. The random encounters can lead to lifelong friendships, but they can also expose the risk, danger, and vulnerability that is climbing, and ultimately, the lack of control we have in putting our lives in someone else's hands.

So it was my friends, Dave and Tim, that laughed their asses off when we came back to camp one day to find that my tent had been destroyed, some of my carrots in the cooler had been eaten, and several beers were crushed and drank.

My heart sank when I saw the sight. My brand-new tent, trampled and crushed to oblivion and the contents of the cooler spilled out into what appeared to me was an act of vandalism. I looked around to find the culprit. Then, I looked to the ground and saw hoof prints. Horses. It was horses.

Dave had an extra tent that he'd scored as booty on Denali the previous year. It was known as the Shit Tent. A client had had some unfortunate bowel occurrences in the tent and left it behind. Dave, being a proper dirtbag, rescued the tent, cleaned it out, and had it as a backup for a situation like this.

Living in the Shit Tent. No wonder I wasn't getting any action during this era. Can you imagine? "Well, would you like to come back to my Shit Tent?" Doesn't exactly flow off the tongue, does it?

The desert can build your spirit up and knock it down. And then, when you're down, it might kick you, as the horses kicked over my cooler and drank my beer. At least there was still beer. And there were still friends. And campfires and stars. The lonely life of a climber living in nature still always has its companions, even if it's just rocks, on the ground and in the sky. This whole planet is just a rock anyways, right? Is it an illusion that we aren't always alone?

In the morning, you're supposed to be excited to climb these cracks again, right? Like that's what you're living for, right? That's what living the dream is? That's what you dreamed about in Outdoor Recreation class when you stared at the teacher and four walls, just waiting to get outside and hit the open road.

Climbing a crack like it's your job becomes a very hard job. These cracks make you feel pain, and they make you bleed, especially if you refused to use tape, as many of us did in those early, stubborn years. "Tape is cheating...tape is aid."

An ideal experience of climbing a crack in the Creek means you gave everything you had, and you were scared and in pain, and when you got to the chains, you'd completed an epic battle; at the top, there would be endorphins flowing through your body, and you'd breathe that fresh desert air, and when you lowered back to the ground, your team would be there to congratulate you on your go, your mojo.

Take the passion out of that equation, and it's a grim picture. When you don't have the strength to do what you've been doing nonstop for the last month. When that desert sun feels like it's beating down on your soul and you're past the point of recovery and you only need a rest day or two, you are burnout, my friend.

That's when it's time to leave. It was hard to accept then because I was never looking beyond the climbing day. What would I do for the summer? I guess I'd go back to that same dishwashing job in Crested Butte and live in a tent again. New tent for sure. I'd get a new tent.

Did I really want to work hard and live in a tent, just to come back to this desert and live in a tent? This is what they called "living the dream," huh? Was I missing something? Why wasn't the desert beautiful and inviting again, like when I arrived? When did the desert become so inhospitable? I would have spit at it had I not been cottonmouthed and burned. Once, the rocks were comforting and inviting, and now all I saw were the sharp thorns of cactuses and horses out to get me.

I would describe the sight in my rearview mirror that hot late-spring day when I left, but I doubt I looked. The only thing in the world that I knew was that I wanted out of the desert, out of that Shit Tent, and back into the mountains, where there were flowers and girls and mountain streams that I could bathe in and sage I could smell deeply and all sorts of other nature comforts that the desert was no longer delivering.

The Pain

The other day, on the Internet, I read about a climber whose fingertip broke off in a crack when he fell. Fingers in a Lightsocket the climb is called, and it's always had a reputation for being fierce, a finger crack that increases in difficulty right up until the last few desperate layback moves. The tag on the story, posted by Mountain Project, was "don't read this at lunch." I'd just had surgery in my mouth (a gum graph), so my stomach was already primed, and I wasn't going to be eating lunch that day anyways because I was on a no-solids diet for a couple days, so I went ahead and looked at it. It was a nightmare come true to us Creek aficionados who jam our limbs in cracks for fun. The climber ended up having part of his finger amputated. The silver lining was that the best big wall climber in the world, Tommy Caldwell, also had a similar injury, losing part of his finger in a home construction accident. So, hopefully this climber will find some inspiration and motivation in knowing he's got an affliction that only briefly slowed down the famous Mr. Caldwell.

There's a derivative of pain, which somehow enhances the experience of a good Indian Creek crack. I've heard and used the word masochism, but still I don't think that encapsulates exactly what the feeling is. It's just a touch of pain, but you don't want the pain to win, just as a boxer might accept some punches, but he or she does not want to get knocked out; they want to be victorious. We want to be victorious. When you clip the chains after a good fight, you don't feel much of the pain—you feel the glory; the pain has been transcended.

A proper enthusiast prepares the body before battle. Off-widths demand the most protection: tape over every exposed section of your hands, high-top shoes that protect your ankles, pants and a long-sleeve shirt, and cams that are bigger than your head. Once you've spent an hour prepping all of that and borrowing cams from everyone at the crag, the battle is the slowest form of free climbing that could be possible. And most stout off-widths rarely have any relief or good rests. It's a full-on battle to the finish.

My "moment" came a few years into a fiendish pursuit of the wide. The full body challenge of a good off-width was hard for me to say no to for a while. The feeling at the end of the battle was so glorious, and the struggle had a seasoned sensation, which elevated every moment into something stupid hard and special.

It was the Big Guy that got me. To the unseasoned, Big Guy is a monster of a line—with eighty-some feet of continuous o-dub climbing, only slightly wavering in width. As every guy or gal who climbs in the Creek knows, there's no generic way to describe a crack; the "size" of a crack is personal and how it corresponds to your body. Problem is, the "normal" way to describe a crack is by the default "man hands"—we refer to climbs as "thin hands" or "a fist crack" based on the average-sized hands of a dude. Getting back to the matter at hand though, Big Guy is a relatively "moderate" off-width for Indian Creek standards, and it's big enough that it's off-width for everyone, unless you were like Shaquille O' Neal or something (probably thin hands for him); it's one I'd climbed a few times previously, while I worked up to my goal of climbing Big Baby, which is a little bit more difficult.

I knew it would be a hard fight, but I knew I had it in me. Plus, I knew the key was climbing efficiently enough until I could get my knee in there. Of the jams one uses in the Creek, the knee is the most surprising the first time you get it. You can almost rest on it, hooking the toe of your foot on the outside of the crack while you weight your entire body on that knee. Before you get the knee, it's desperado— hand stacks and heel-toes—but once you get that knee, it gives you a chance to breathe.

So there I am, jamming along, getting worked, but making slow upward progress, and then I try to move and I can't. I breathe and try again. Nothing. After a minute of this personal panic, I yell down to Shaun, my belayer, "My knee is stuck."

"I was wondering what the hell you were doing up there," he jokingly yells back, while I'm trying self-talk to keep calm.

The panic pulses like my heartbeat, leaving me momentarily and then coming back, making me think bad thoughts. The paranoia ricochets and reverberates between these two thoughts: my knee is stuck; I must free my knee. I'm looking to Shaun for some guidance, but there's not really much he can say. "Did you try moving it upward? Does it feel looser?"

I mumble something back each time, and with each passing minute, I'm getting more scared. I'd heard about a woman getting her knee stuck in Escalante Canyon a little while ago, and she had to be rescued out of there with a pulley system, resulting in some serious knee injuries. A stuck knee was the last thing I had in my mind when I went up this climb, which was supposed to be routine.

Then, for what seemed like an eternity, I moved my knee in a different direction and it slid out—just like that. I aided my way to the top.

A year later at a book signing at Mountainfilm in Telluride, I met the woman who had to be rescued out of S Crack in Escalante Canyon, a place often described as Colorado's Mini Indian Creek. It was also one of the places I cut my teeth as a trad climber, a seemingly haunted but stunning little canyon, carved into an otherwise desolate landscape.

She told me about the rescue, of the hours that she hung there, the subsequent removal of her knee, and the aftermath of the injury inflicted upon it. She was embarrassed by the incident. I tried to explain how I could understand, but a few minutes with a stuck knee is nothing like having a rescue team come to your assistance.

You just kind of think that thing is really never going to happen to anyone. You also think that you'd never lose a finger to a crack, but these things happen, in the inviting yet unforgiving place we simply call The Desert.

And, now all I can think of is that guy's fingertip, still possibly up there in the crack, waiting for his buddies to come along and pluck it out.

The Next Generation

Well, the first days are the hardest days

Don't you worry anymore

When life looks like easy street

There is danger at your door

—The Grateful Dead, "Uncle John's Band"

This young hippie left a bag of his groceries with my stuff after last weekend climbing in the Creek—granola, ramen, tortillas—you know, the usual, standard fare. Same stuff I was eating fifteen years ago when I was a young, idealistic, over-stoker bohemian type.

We'd invited a couple of our younger friends along for the adventure of sampling some new routes, and they invited a few of their friends, so it was kinda this big hippie adventure.

From my perspective, hippie or not, there are only two types of young climbers: the cocky ones who don't want your advice or help, and the other, more humble types, the ones who sense that climbing is this adventure thing that you take a big bite off of, more than you can chew, and then you sort it out as you go along. Fortunately, this crew all fell in the latter category.

We older climbers are scarce when compared to the masses that are joining our culture of cliff dancing. Yeah, it's cliff dancing out here in the desert, 'cause it ain't no damn sport—most of the time we just sit around and look at how beautiful it is, but beautiful is not the right word: it's sublime; it's something we *NEED*, not something we can do without once we know it.

But they (you) barely know it, and once it's tasted, more is desired. This is where souls come to heal and get bruised at the same time, but you know it's the body that is bruised, not the spirit. The spirit is invigorated here.

And there is poetry here, and they (you) know it all instinctually. But what you don't know instinctually is how to climb in this place, how to protect it, and how to treat it right. That's where we come in. We've learned. Sometimes the hard way. I know there are plenty of times when I did the wrong thing, when I got off trail, or when I didn't pack out my poop. But you know, we make these mistakes, and then we try to share the information so that we're not all making these mistakes all the time. The desert is a precious place. And at this moment in time, when we are preoccupied with digital technology, the desert speaks supreme truths about our souls. It helps us protect our souls.

When I hear of climbing and the next generation, it's always in the terms of sport and athleticism. What about aesthetics? What about climbing as art? What about climbing as life? What about climbing as love? What about climbing as an escape from this industry that wants us glued to our phones? And where do they learn this?

And what the hell do I know about answers? I'm still searching, and I'm learning that a lot of answers just probably don't come until old age, or death. And even though I'm approaching forty years old, that number doesn't seem old or wise anymore.

I can only know what I see in them and the few things I'm able to teach them. Yes, you should get a helmet. No, don't get into that bowline knot; sure it works, but is it fail proof like the Figure 8? Yes, you do need a bigger pack, especially for these Indian Creek days. Tape is good; it protects from the gobies, because it's bad style to bleed all over a route, and you'll last longer if you protect your skin. Water is good too. So is beer if you can handle yourself, but save it for the end of the day.

Sunsets, yeah sunsets at the Creek are the best. Don't you just wish you could fade away with it sometimes? But like Neil Young said, it's better to burn out than fade away. I guess. Do you guys still listen to Neil Young and Bob Dylan and The Dead? Cool. Yeah, I thought you did.

You're not all hippies though. I get it. I just have a romantic notion toward hippieness 'cause that's where I started. But, I hope you're different than mainstream America, 'cause mainstream sucks. It's boring. It's not doing good things for America. It's why we have Trump and TVs that are on all the time, and how do you even think with a TV on all the time? How do you think different thoughts? I've pondered this a lot, and my only answer is to disconnect and be Out There. Or Out Here. But even those moments that I'm drawing upon from yesterday that were simple and beautiful are now the past.

The next generation, I probably have more to offer you in writing and stories than I do with us climbing together. I can only share a rope with so few of you. I can only warn so few of you in person how high the stakes are in climbing.

That climbing wants to kill you. It really does.

It's like that spider, I forget which one, that mates with its prey and then kills and eats it. Climbing isn't plastic or pretty, or even sexy most of the time. It's dirty and dark and secretive until you've paid your dues by almost losing your life. And, even then, it takes your friends to the next climb, that thing called death. But, it's everything too, especially in this world gone crazy that gets crazier every day. Climbing brings us to nature, and that is where we came from, so yeah, that's why this lifestyle feels so good.

Social media, and the media in general, promises that your generation will take the grades higher and the objectives bigger. Shit, maybe someday someone will even free solo El Capitan. I'm sure that all will happen—evolution in our sport is predictable even if it's still mind blowing. While the world awaits V17, I know most of you will be chuffing through your experiences like outdoor climbers have always done and will always do, sharing sunsets and sips of water, preparing for that perfect moment on that perfect climb, that place and moment in time that is all yours, on this ball of rock hurling through space.

New Routes

Oh baby I like it raw,

Yeah baby I like it raw

—Ol' Dirty Bastard,
"Shimmy Shimmy Ya"

It's a fine line between work and play when developing a new splitter crack. Of course that crack isn't new; it's been there longer than you and will remain long after our spark of existence that we call a lifetime. But, to uncover one, to climb and clean it, is satisfying, in both a blue-collar and dirtbag way.

I'd dabbled in granite new-route development for a decade or so, starting with hand drilling at the local crag up in Gunnison and finally borrowing a power drill whenever one of the older climbers would let me. It's hard to mess up on granite; the rock is so good, and it always takes a bolt.

Sandstone is different. It's easy to drill a sketchy bolt in sandstone. I've taken bolts out by hand at anchors on popular routes in Indian Creek. Usually, it's because of an intense direction of pull on the bolts, but sometimes it's just because it's shitty, hollow rock. Bottom line is that you trust the first ascentionist quite a bit when using their anchor bolts.

Our crew began putting up new routes after we'd regularly armed ourselves with drills for anchor replacement at the crags. For a while there, it was guaranteed that you would find an anchor on a popular route that needed some love. So we pretty much always started climbing up with a drill and bolts. Inevitably, on the edges of popular crags, you can find some unclimbed cracks.

A few cracks just need a quick brushing, and they are good to go. These are the rare ones, especially in the modern context of Indian Creek. The obvious splitters were established years ago. The leftovers aren't too shabby; they just demand more elbow grease.

Most Creek climbs have to go ground up, not necessarily out of a tradition to ethics but out of necessity. Occasionally, you can get "two for one" by climbing a nearby crack and then swinging over and cleaning its neighbor. That's a good technique when a death block looms above your head, and you don't want to delicately dance around it all for the sake of a new line.

Ultimately, though, you'll be climbing on something that just an hour later you'll pry off with a crowbar. But sandstone typically makes sense, and a loose pillar can usually hold body weight—you hope, at least.

They say that the granite on El Capitan is like an onion, and it comes off in layers, exfoliating in time. If that's the case, then the sandstone of Indian Creek is kinda like Jenga, blocks that aren't attached and can be cleaned with the proper tools, like a hammer and a crowbar.

It's often dusty, so I carry a bandana in my back pocket and sometimes even ski goggles. Often, a battle with a loose block can last up to an hour. It's you versus the rock. With the really big ones, your only real tool is the crowbar. You just have to move the block enough so that gravity will accept it and trundle it down the hill. It's an inches game, and with every inch you move it, you've got to make sure the block won't catch onto the rope when it finally is broken loose. When it eventually does go careening down the hillside, you just hope it didn't fuck up a chipmunk's day or any other wildlife just having a fine day in the sun when this massive chunk of sandstone comes a-crashing.

Another fun phenomenon in the Creek is the mud-filled crack. Some cracks are just funnels for storms, and while they look sexy and perfect, in reality they are dirty and flawed. That's when it's time to really roll up the sleeves and get to work. One climb out at the Creek that we dubbed Ol' Dirty Bastard, after the famous Wu-Tang rapper, was so dirty it took hours upon hours to hammer the mud out of the crack with a crowbar. It was one of those climbs when you just wished you'd never started because of how much cleaning it required.

In the end, the best part of a first ascent at the Creek is establishing something that will push you to try your absolute hardest, a line that will leave you sleepless at night, obsessing over the moves, and one day, after countless attempts, will finally go and leave you contented, for the moment.

Future

As I write these words, the future of this place we humans now call Indian Creek is up in the balance. All of the sources I know confirm that Obama is going to sign the Bears Ears National Monument, thus changing the status of the land that is the Creek. How exactly that will affect climbing is unknown, but it will protect the land from development, or at least we can only hope it will do that. From what I hear, people are proposing rollercoasters in the Grand Canyon and changing the names of things in Yosemite. It's hard to keep up with it all.

For all I know, we could be living in a Trump world by the time this book is published. I'm scared of that, for sure. Republicans don't fight to protect the land; they fight to develop it. But, of course, that guy is not your average Republican. Kinda seems worse in a lot of ways.

I know the birds won't know the difference. Or the coyotes. Or the crag dogs. Well, maybe the crag dogs, if dogs aren't allowed there anymore. We'll see.

I like the land the way it is now, BLM land where you're basically free to move around as a climber without overbearing rules and regulations. But you know what, I don't know how much my opinion really matters. What matters most is that the organization that fights for us, the Access Fund, gets my support, and they advocate the policies that will be best for climbers. There's a long history of compromise and conservation out in Indian Creek, and the best thing for the land now is protection, well, as far as I can see it at the moment.

I can't imagine my life without Indian Creek, without that land. I'd have to go on Prozac or something—the desert medicine is necessary to my soul.

When the world drives me crazy, with all the unhinged people and all the violence that we can't seem to escape, Indian Creek makes me feel sane again. Sometimes I never want to leave, but of course, everyone always has to leave to refuel and resupply. I imagine even the ranchers who live there go to the grocery store. Sometimes I envsion spending more and more time out there, but then I realize I need to make a living, and I don't want to go back to the days when I lived out of a vehicle. It's just not me. Not right now.

But I like the fantasy, and these days the days seem to go by so fast. My spirit never wants to leave. And I guess it doesn't because here I am, typing away, drifting, back to the Creek.

Always, like always, it's about the climbing. Those are the best moments, and when you think of the grand scale of time and the history of climbing, Indian Creek becomes so exciting and fresh because it is so new. No, we aren't the first group of climbers; any research on the ancient people of the red rock lands will show that they reached perches and places that demanded climbing. I mean, look at the cliff dwellings in Mesa Verde! There was some fifth-class X-rated climbing going on, for sure.

Recently there's been a surge of bouldering going on in Indian Creek. At first, I thought it was a couple novelty roadside problems, but hearing about what's going on, it seems like it's this cool adventure bouldering thing, and they've established hundreds of problems throughout the Indian Creek corridor. I've yet to sample any of the bouldering, but already, it's opened my mind to more creative thinking out at a place that so far has mostly only developed the splitter cracks for climbing.

Chris Schulte has been at the forefront of this development, and he's also responsible for most of the writing that has been done. Recently, he reflected on the tunnel vision of only looking for splitters in Indian Creek and what happened to him in the process of bouldering and thinking outside the box (or the crack): "You've heard that tired, old phrase about *taking the skills learned on the boulders/cliffs to the cliffs/big walls*, and it rings true here in the desert. Once again, the broad promise of the future is all around us, for the Creek has new runout routes that abandon the cracks and quest up grips and geometry. The Creek has 5.15 arêtes and 5.11 slabs."

That statement right there just makes me want to quit writing about this place and pack up the Subaru to be there. All good things in all good time, I guess. I'll be back there soon enough. Somehow, that place has consumed me entirely, and it's the only place I really want to climb these days. That may change with the rules and regulation, and someday I may lament the changes and talk about the good old days. But the good old days still seem to be at hand in the desert.

The stillness of the desert, the azure of the sky, the contrast of the red rock with everything else, it makes me think about things in a different way; it makes me feel different. Lately, I find myself worrying about the world, a lot, and I probably should. I find solace and comfort in an uncomfortable place, with a community of people that are hungry for the same thing I am hungry for, and a desire for peace that I can't seem to attain in the modern world.

Change. Change. Change. It's all the world does. Indian Creek will change too. It once used to be an ocean. Perspective on the cliffs will change too; excitement is really high in the air right now. I hope that respect for the land is high too—how can we give back to a place that gives us so much in such a quiet way? The answer is out there.

Check out more of Mehall's writing at:

www.lukemehall.com

www.climbingzine.com

About the author

Luke Mehall lives in Durango, Colorado. He is the publisher of *The Climbing Zine*, an independent print publication, and he is the author of *American Climber*, *The Great American Dirtbags*, and *Climbing Out of Bed*. He enjoys climbing, sleeping in tents, hip-hop, yoga, and uninterrupted mornings of writing. He believes in the power of independent media and too-soon poetry. He can be contacted at luke@climbingzine.com.

Made in the USA
Charleston, SC
19 December 2016